PRAISE FOR THE PEOPLE OF BUSIN

D1507100

The People Side of Business provides a roadmap for understanding people in the workplace. What a cogent synthesis of psychological science for leaders in business!

Ron Levant, PhD, Past President, American Psychological Association; Professor of Psychology, The University of Akron

Hersch and DeMaio have integrated a great deal of contemporary neuroscience and pragmatic leadership theory in a narrative about Dominion Medical Center and the new CEO Dr. Charles Fisher as he attempts to enrich the people side of his organization. Each of the chapters illuminates one of the six principles that must be deployed in order to build a high-performing organization. The narrative and the framing of the principles provide valuable insights for the reader.

Alexander B. Horniman, Killgallon Ohio Art Professor of Business Administration, Darden School of Business, University of Virginia

The People Side of Business is a must read for business leaders who desire to maximize long-term business performance. DeMaio and Hersch's key principles recognize the importance and impact of people within an organization and provide the leadership tools to satisfy the employee's emotional and developmental needs within the modern business structure, ultimately leading to the desired culture and total organizational success.

James Quarforth, Retired Chairman and CEO, NTELOS Holdings Corp

DeMaio and Hersch are clearly onto something with their concept of a "third domain" of organizational excellence. As an academic and practicing organizational improvement consultant, I often encounter senior managers who are impressive in their technical expertise and/or business acumen, but who have yet to understand (or even notice) the people side of the organization: work culture, interpersonal values and behaviors, human motivation, and psychology. As a result, they often fail to address their "social architecture" responsibilities: the need to create an environment that causes people to develop their full potential that presents challenging work in a supportive work culture, and that creates a structured framework that encourages team-based autonomy and commitment to a purpose beyond themselves. This third domain is one of the most important keys to building high-performance organizations – and one of the most neglected. I found the use of the story/case approach to presenting their material very effective; it made the six psychological principles featured in the book all the more accessible.

John W. Pickering, Ph.D President, Commonwealth Center for High-Performance Organizations, Former Deputy Director at the US Office of Personnel Managements' Federal Executive Institute

"As an executive coach and organization development consultant for more than 40 years for Fortune 500 companies, I have often wished I had a book like "The People Side of Business" to give to my clients. Many had read the latest books on leadership, motivation, and organizational excellence. Too many of those books lacked what Drs. DeMaio and Hersch convincingly provide: a set of principles for executives that align with the brain's core motivational drivers to help them create and sustain optimal organizational performance and health."

Ralph Bates, President, Bates and Associates.

The Third Domain of Organizational Excellence:
The People Side of Business

Thomas J. DeMaio, Ph.D.

and

Lee E. Hersch, Ph.D.

To order a copy of this book, visit:
www.CreateSpace.com/3670963
www.Amazon.com
Other bookselling retailers.

ISBN-13: 9781470165192
ISBN-10: 1470165198

Library of Congress Control Number: 2012906379
CreateSpace, North Charleston, SC

TABLE OF CONTENTS

PREFACE

There is no one idea, no simple solution, no silver bullet for building the people side of an organization. It requires an overarching, holistic perspective on human psychology, one that recognizes the predictable needs that shape behavior and experience. The most common reason for businesses failing to maximize the power of their most precious resource—their employee's dedication and creativity—is that their leaders have a partial understanding of how these needs and desires affect people in the work environment.

This is not surprising. Although most executives possess a sophisticated grasp of industry dynamics, they often lack a similar comprehensive framework to apply to the people side of business. One reason is that the science behind this is very new. The other is that such a comprehensive framework hasn't been readily available. We wrote this book to fill this gap. We've distilled the latest knowledge into six principles that, when taken together, can help leaders understand why people act the way they do in the work environment and what they can do to shape those reactions for optimum performance.

Our purpose here is to help readers maximize the performance of their organizations. This is not a book about workplace therapy. It's about using a fundamental understanding of psychology to build a more flexible, more resourceful, and ultimately a more successful business.

Rather than simply listing our principles, we decided to depict how they might play out in a typical enterprise, focusing on the experiences of a new CEO in a highly competitive industry. With the assistance of Charlie Feigenoff, we created a fictional business—in this case, a hospital—that we've filled with composites of characters that we've met scores of times during our consultations. Their counterparts may be working for you. Though our story is set in a hospital, for us it's just a convenient setting for illustrating the process of focusing an enterprise on the people side of business. At the end of each chapter, we summarize each principle for later reference.

In addition to reflecting the latest scientific knowledge, this book is based on our years of work with clinical and business clients. We are indebted to them for what they have taught us. We also greatly appreciate the care with which friends and family read our drafts and commented on our ideas.

CAST OF CHARACTERS

Dr. Charles Fisher – Chief Executive Officer

Dr. Ryan Albert – Medical Director, Chief of Oncology

Bob Bishop – Chief Operating Officer (Former interim CEO)

Jim Hawthorne – Former Chief Executive Officer

Debbie Smith – Director of Nursing

Henry Powell – Chief Financial Officer

Barry Johnson – Vice President for Information Technology

Julie Martinez - Vice President for Marketing

Sally Heally - Vice President of Human Resources

Lee Hersch – Organizational Consultant

Tom DeMaio – Organizational Consultant

Dr. Lou Perrott - Chief of Surgery

Dr. Andy Benjamin – Chief of Orthopedics

Joyce Williams – Nurse, not promoted, filed complaint

Dan Welch – Staff in Billing Department

Shannon Heinzmann – Operating Room Nurse

Dr. Mark Bartholomew – Surgeon

Jack Farina – Staff in Information Technology

PROLOGUE

The sun had been up just 15 minutes when Dr. Charles Fisher drove into the parking lot at Dominion Medical Center. As he stepped out of his car, he could tell it was going to be another scorcher, not that it mattered to him. He would be in the building until early evening. The excitement of being the new CEO had yet to wear off, and Charlie liked getting to the hospital early and talking to the staff as they settled into the day shift. Then he devoted the hour or two before his assistant arrived to catching up on e-mail, tackling one or two small projects, and thinking through the morning's meetings. In the three months he had been on the job, he had come to relish this quiet, creative time. True, it meant going to bed really early, but he was starting to like that too.

Today was going to be different, though. He had called an emergency meeting of the executive team for 7:00 a.m.

Yesterday morning, the hospital's medical director had stopped by his office with disturbing news. "I hate to tell you this," said Dr. Ryan Albert, handing him a neatly bound report. "The Quality Assurance Committee has crunched the latest numbers. What had seemed the last two months like a one-time uptick now looks like a definite trend: the incidence of MRSA is on the rise."

As a hospital administrator and physician, Charlie immediately knew the hospital had a serious problem on its hands.

1

The Third Domain of Organizational Excellence

Methicillin-resistant Staphylococcus aureus, known to the medical community as MRSA, is a truly nasty bug. It can enter the body through the slightest break in the skin, producing painful abscesses and traveling through the bloodstream to attack the joints, lungs, and heart. Unchecked, MRSA can be deadly.

The key to containing MRSA is to test all patients on admission, rigorously isolating any patient with the infection, and using one of the few remaining antibiotics that can still knock it out. Hospital staff members treating a person with MRSA also have to gown up before going into a patient's room. That's the first line of defense. The second is to make sure that all staff members wash their hands before they touch a patient— no exceptions.

Charlie realized, this was clearly a people problem, as so many quality control issues are, not just a medical problem. Everyone at Dominion knew the correct procedures, and they knew how important it was to be scrupulous about following them. Somehow, though, there was a disconnect. The staff members simply weren't being as careful as they needed to be. Charlie decided to call an emergency meeting to get some insight from his executive team about what was going on. He also wanted them to take a close look at the financial and operational implications for the hospital and to develop a plan together to contain and eliminate the infection.

Scheduling a meeting to formulate Dominion's response turned out to be unexpectedly difficult. All through the afternoon, Charlie's administrative assistant worked his e-mail with increasing frustration. When he thought he had found a time that worked for the majority of the team, there were always a few holdouts claiming they had department meetings they just couldn't postpone. This was puzzling to Charlie. Didn't they understand they had an urgent hospital-wide problem on their hands? Finally, Charlie just gave up. He had his assistant tell everyone to come in early for a 7:00 a.m. meeting. He didn't like getting involved in things like scheduling, and he particularly wasn't crazy about surrendering one of his early-morning hours, but the hospital's core mission—its ability to deliver care—was at stake. People come to hospitals to get better, not to get sick.

As Charlie walked into the conference room, he noted that it was unusually quiet and that everyone was looking at him expectantly. This was the first crisis of his tenure, and he knew that people were curious about how he would respond. Charlie was ready for that—but he wasn't prepared for the way the meeting unfolded.

He began by asking Ryan to report on the latest Quality Assurance Committee findings. Ryan had hardly had a chance to gather his notes and sit down when Bob Bishop, the hospital's COO, jumped in. Bob had served as the interim director after Jim Hawthorne, the long-term CEO, resigned suddenly after his diagnosis with cancer. Charlie appreciated the good grace with which Bob had welcomed him when he came on board. He knew that Bob had hoped to become the permanent CEO, and he respected Bob's deep commitment to the hospital. Bob had reached the same conclusion about the root of the MRSA infection that Charlie had, though the anger and frustration in Bob's voice took Charlie by surprise.

"I've said over and over that we've become too complacent, but no one seemed to be listening," Bob began. "People know the procedures. I just don't understand why they don't follow them. We know that infection control is all about hand hygiene, about paying attention to the little things that keep everyone safe. It's not rocket science, for Pete's sake. We need to make sure all employees—especially the nurses—are held accountable for following these procedures," he said, jabbing at the table with his forefinger for emphasis. "And we need to demonstrate to the staff that there will be consequences if we can't get a grip on this epidemic."

The director of nursing, Debbie Smith, looked stunned. She turned to Bob, her voice shaking, "If you don't think this outbreak is upsetting to me, you're mistaken. My staff is working on MRSA control all the time. I talk to them about hand washing day in and day out, so I think it's very unfair to single out nursing. After all, the physicians, the lab, and the housekeeping staff could be at fault too."

Bob was about to reply when Henry Powell, the CFO and longest-serving member of the executive team, interrupted. "You both can bicker all you want about the cause of the outbreak, but from my point of view, the consequences to our bottom line are the same. Do you have any idea how much it costs to isolate a patient?" he asked looking pointedly across the table at Debbie. "Budgets are tight. We need a solution, and we need one now!"

"That's right," added Barry Johnson, the young vice president for IT who typically sat next to Henry. "Here we are, working to make the transition to an electronic medical record system, and we're going to be jeopardizing the whole project by diverting money to fight MRSA. At this rate, our competitors are going to eat our lunch."

Across the table, Julie Martinez, the vice president for marketing, looked like she couldn't believe what she was hearing. "You know, Barry," she hissed, "if you could get a grip on your programmers, we would have plenty of money to deal with MRSA. We've already sunk hundreds of thousands of dollars into the EMR system, and we have precious little to show for it. If you want to talk about underperforming staff, you don't have to look far."

Barry just sat there, looking smug. "If you only knew how complicated an EMR install can be, you would understand," he said.

But before he could go on, Julie was back on the attack. "I'll tell you what I do know," she said furiously. "I know that if I had your budget, this hospital would be at full capacity all the time."

Charlie had heard more than enough. Certainly, the executive team consisted of capable, hard-working professionals who were committed to the well-being of Dominion's patients. They were perfectly cordial, though maybe a bit reserved, when nothing was at stake. Under pressure, their veneer of collegiality quickly peeled off. From Charlie's perspective, this discussion, if you could call it that, was little more than a turf war.

"Can we get the conversation back to MRSA?" he asked impatiently. "I understand that it costs money to fight MRSA, and that's another reason to get on top of this outbreak." Henry nodded his head. "And I agree with Bob that the underlying cause is people." Now it was Bob's turn to beam. "But I wouldn't lay the blame at the feet of the nursing staff," he added. "It strikes me that the MRSA outbreak reflects a system-wide problem." Debbie looked both relieved and grateful.

Sally Heally, the vice president of human resources, had been following the conversation intently. Now she spoke up. "I don't know if this is related, but for the last six months or so, I've been trying to tell you all that something is up with the staff, but no one here seemed particularly interested. People have always liked working at Dominion, but lately turnover has been on the rise—and we're losing people we would like to keep. Exit interviews have also started to take on a negative tone. People are telling us they don't feel appreciated."

"Well, if they can't take the simple steps required to deal with MRSA, they're not going to be appreciated," said Bob judgmentally. "We need to hold them accountable."

Charlie stepped in before the argument took off again. "If we agree on one thing, it's that we can contain MRSA if we can somehow reach our people," he said, looking around the room. "I'm going to ask Sally to work with Ryan to head up our response. After all, reaching people is her area of expertise. I need a plan by the end of the week. And I want you both to reach out to the rest of the executive team and report back to me on the financial, operational, and public relations implications of this problem. This was something I was hoping to get to this morning, but that's clearly not in the cards. Let's pull together and get ahead of the outbreak right now."

If Charlie had been hoping for an enthusiastic reaction, he was disappointed. Bob and Henry simply looked sullenly at the table. Barry sat spinning a paper clip with a bored expression on his face. And Debbie and Julie eyed him suspiciously, as if trying to figure out his real motive. Only Ryan and Sally seemed truly energized by the way he handled the problem.

"Okay folks, we all have things to do," Charlie said, on his way out of the room. Glancing at his watch, he said, "Bob, will you drop by at around eight or so? I'd like to talk a few things over with you."

Back at the office, Charlie stood next to the leather chair that had belonged to his predecessor, Jim Hawthorne, a little more than a year ago and stared out into the parking lot. "It seems I have a real problem on my hands," he thought to himself, though deep down he was not surprised. Board certified in family medicine, Charlie had seen plenty of dysfunctional families in his time, and he had thought he recognized these symptoms at Dominion. As the newly minted CEO, Charlie made regular rounds of the departments throughout the hospital. It was his way of meeting his staff, learning the culture, and making himself both visible and accessible. He had noticed that the hospital staff was by and large pleased to see him and eager to share their views, but they were also standoffish. Sure, the staff seemed invested in taking care of their patients and in the success of their own departments, but he had no sense that anyone focused that much on Dominion as a whole.

He saw the same problem on his executive team. A committed group of leaders, they were articulate advocates for their own areas of responsibility, each making his or her case for resources. In fact, he had detailed funding proposals on his desk from each of department heads. They were all reasonable, but there was no overall vision. They liked going their separate ways, so much so that they even had a hard time finding time to meet.

Putting it all together, it was not surprising he had a MRSA outbreak. He had many people working diligently without really

7

communicating with each other—or even being interested in cooperating. For all his education and experience, Charlie didn't know what to do.

After he completed his residency, Charlie had gone on to earn an MBA degree. For him, understanding large complex organizations like hospitals had the same attraction as understanding the human body. It was another fascinating system to master, and he enjoyed applying the management tools he had learned at business school in positions of ever-greater responsibility at hospitals around the country. Now he was getting the chance to run his own show—but somehow after all that experience and study he still lacked the tools to make the people side of his organization healthy. He was going to have to do something about that.

There was a knock at the door. Charlie glanced up and noticed Bob standing there. It was eight on the dot. He invited Bob to come in. As he did once again, Charlie marveled at Bob's good grace. Bob had sat in Jim's chair while the hospital board made its decision to choose Charlie, rather than him, yet he never treated the office as if he had any claim to it. Charlie knew this was not particularly because Bob felt any deference to him, personally. It was just that Bob, in his own way, loved Dominion. An ex-Marine, Bob believed in service.

Bob and Charlie settled in around Charlie's table. "Bob, I'm beginning to think that the MRSA outbreak is just the tip of the iceberg. What's your thinking?" Charlie said, deliberately leaving the request vague, just to see how Bob would respond.

"I couldn't agree more," Bob replied. "As far as I'm concerned, the MRSA outbreak is really a symptom of what's happening all over Dominion. It all comes down to a fundamental lack of accountability. Under Jim, we did pretty well. Jim was always committed to quality care, though he was not one for policy and procedure. Most of the follow-up fell to me." Bob stopped for a second and adjusted his glasses.

"When Jim was diagnosed with cancer and had to resign, it came as quite a shock to us all. When the board appointed me interim CEO, I felt the best way to deal with losing Jim was for us to buckle down and work harder instead of feeling sorry for ourselves. I immediately set ambitious quality goals for each department and outlined detailed procedures to ensure the staff met them. In addition, I instituted reporting methods, based on quantifiable metrics, to create the accountability that was lacking during Jim's tenure."

"Now don't get me wrong," Bob added after a second. "Jim was a great leader, and I learned a lot from him. But while being personable might have worked fine in the past, it is my view that we should employ management tools that produce measurable results. I'll be the first to admit that I'm a bit baffled that things didn't work out the way they should have. I set clear goals, so I thought I was making things easy, but we always fell short of expectations. And I didn't get much cooperation from the rest of the executive team. They just never really got behind the idea of accountability."

Charlie looked at Bob, who seemed genuinely puzzled by his failure. With his military bearing and sharply pressed dark suit, Bob was, Charlie thought, a force to be reckoned with—although he looked a little lonely. Bob did things by the numbers, and he expected the numbers to add up. When they didn't, he redoubled his efforts. Charlie couldn't quite put his finger on it, but he was sure that Bob had played a role in the people issues that were undermining Dominion.

After Bob left, Charlie wandered over to his desk and sat down in Jim's chair. As he looked around the office, it occurred to him that Jim had not only imposed his vision on Dominion, but had left his mark on the room—and Charlie had to admit Jim had a certain verve, both as an administrator and as a decorator. At a time when hundreds of hospitals were closing, Jim had brought Dominion into the twenty-first century and had put it on a sound financial footing. His office was somehow both modern and comfortable.

In the year since Jim had resigned, neither Charlie nor Bob had done much to change it. Bob added a metal table and a computer. Jim had never learned to use a computer, though he had purchased hundreds of them for the hospital, and had hired Barry. Charlie had brought in a collection of his favorite management books and a generous assortment of family pictures, but on consideration still felt a bit like a guest.

Charlie sat there for a few minutes, and then made a decision. He picked up the phone and gave Sally Heally, Dominion's vice president for human resources, a call. After asking her if there was anything he could do to help her with her MRSA plan, he got down to his real reason for calling. "Sally, I appreciated your speaking up at this morning's meeting," he said. "And you were absolutely spot on; it's people, not medical expertise, that's at the root of the difficulties we're having at Dominion. I just don't know how to get a handle on the problem so I can figure out what to do about it. I'd like to call in some outside help to give us a thorough workup and some fresh ideas. I need to find a way to bring us all together in the most productive way possible before things really get out of control. Do you have any suggestions?"

Sally thought for a second. "I've heard good things about a firm called HerschDeMaio Associates," she said. The two principals, Lee Hersch and Tom DeMaio, have worked with many different companies and nonprofits over the years. They're clinical psychologists and organizational consultants. My understanding is that they've been developing a framework they call "the people side of business." The managers I know who have worked with them said their ideas made a lot of sense and their framework helped them understand what was going on in their organizations and develop a plan to address their problems.

"That sounds interesting," Charlie said, although he was still feeling noncommittal.

"The people I know also said that Tom and Lee are not the kind of consultants that run through a PowerPoint, drop off a report, and leave. Their approach is to explain their framework and use it to help management come up with a strategy that fits the needs of the organization. Best of all, they'll stick with you until you feel the problem is resolved."

"That's more like it," Charlie thought. "Sally, why don't you do a little checking? If they turn out to be as promising as you've heard, get back to me so I can find time to meet with them, the sooner the better."

CHAPTER 1

THE DESIGN OF THE BRAIN DETERMINES HUMAN BEHAVIOR

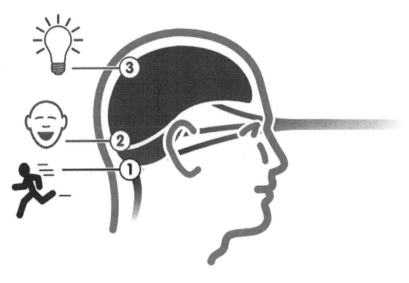

Two weeks later, when Charlie's assistant ushered Lee Hersch and Tom DeMaio into Charlie's office, Charlie was more than ready to get started. With a few minor tweaks, he had adopted Sally Heally's and Ryan Albert's turnaround plan for MRSA, and now it was just a matter of waiting a few weeks for the Quality Assurance Committee's next report. But everything he had seen in the interim had convinced him that the MRSA outbreak was just symptomatic of a larger issue. He needed to get a grip on the people issues that were beginning to undermine Dominion's performance. As an institution, Dominion was beginning to fray. He was hoping that these two consultants, Hersch and DeMaio, could help him mend it.

The Third Domain of Organizational Excellence

They shook hands and settled around his conference table. "I noticed as we came in that you have quite a library of business classics," said Lee, nodding at Charlie's bookshelves. Lee seemed the more conservative of the two, with his tweed jacket, button-down shirt, and striped tie. "I noticed some Peter Drucker and John Maxwell on your shelves."

"I like to keep some of the business books that have made an impression on me within reach," Charlie said, "though at this point, it's hard for me to find the time to read more than a chapter at a time. *First, Break All the Rules*; *Good to Great*; *Hardwiring Excellence*; *Results That Last*; *Emotional Intelligence*; and the rest have all helped me think in new ways about leadership." As they talked more, Charlie found that the two shared his enthusiasm for many of these titles, not only for the books' insight into business issues, but also because they shed light on what Lee and Tom called "the people side of business."

Charlie liked what he heard, but he still wanted to know more before making a commitment. "Before we get started," he said, "why don't you tell me a bit about yourselves and how you work?"

Tom and Lee looked at each other, and then Lee began, "The first thing to keep in mind is that we're both organizational consultants and psychologists. We've worked with hundreds of individuals over the years, but our real focus is extending our understanding of people to companies and nonprofits. The one thing that every organization has in common is that they are all, ultimately, groups of individuals. Accordingly, leaders who want to make their organizations as efficient and productive as possible must understand why people act the way they do."

"Our role is to assess the people side of your organization, share with you the information you need to get the most out of your people, and help you use that information to formulate a plan," added Tom. "After all, you're the physician with the MBA and years of executive experience."

"Fair enough," Charlie said, grinning. "I see you've done a little digging yourselves."

"Better dig now than to have to dig out later if we don't gel," Tom replied. "When we start a project, we want to be reasonably confident that we're working with someone with a real commitment to fundamental change."

"I think I qualify," said Charlie. "From what I've seen in the few months I've been at Dominion, we have to change. Either we transform the culture of this place or Dominion is going to suffer. We're doing amazingly well, considering that the members of my executive team seem to place their own departments before the well-being of the hospital, and my COO, with the best of intentions, responds to crises by ratcheting up the pressure on everyone and insisting on ever-higher standards. But I have a sense that the status quo is just not sustainable. The reports I'm getting from HR show that we're starting to lose some very good employees. Because what you call *the people side of business* seems so intangible, most of my top executives don't even recognize the people issues we face, and those that do— with a few exceptions—dismiss them."

Charlie paused for a second. "You mentioned that I'm a physician. The way I look at it, my medical training gives me a window into the quality of our services. With one major exception that I'll talk to you about in a second, we're doing pretty well. At the same time, my MBA allows me to understand the fiscal and business situation here at Dominion. Generally, we are in pretty good shape here, too. Of course, there is always a lot to be done, but there's a sense that things are starting to unravel.

"For my part, I'm clear about what I need to accomplish. I'm just stymied by the people issues. What I need is a PhD in psychology. Since I don't exactly have a lot of free time these days, I thought the next best thing would be to bring you two guys in."

Now it was Tom and Lee's turn to smile. Charlie seemed genuinely interested in getting to the root of the problems that Dominion was having, not looking for some superficial fix.

"We're with you," Tom said. "In simple terms, companies that are successful over the long haul require expertise in three areas: the business domain, which requires strong fiscal planning and management; the technical domain, in your case, quality medical care; and then there's the people domain. All three areas are critical to the success of any organization. The people side is the area most often shortchanged, seen as a luxury that's peripheral to business success. But here's the rub: if you don't pay attention to the people side, you'll fall short on the business and technical sides. Sure, companies can do pretty well for a while by focusing on the first two, but these days 'pretty well' isn't good enough and it's certainly not great."

A History of Dominion

"Exactly," Charlie said, "so let me tell you what's going on here." Charlie looked down at the table, gathering his thoughts.

"When Jim Hawthorne arrived here 20 years ago, Dominion was a small medical center in a small market, but Jim was clearly one of those administrators who could see change coming. He sensed the region was growing and that Dominion had a chance to become a true health system. Slowly but surely he transformed this place.

"Jim was a persuasive recruiter, bringing in a group of topnotch young physicians. He worked with Henry Powell, our CFO, to make sure that there was money in the budget for investment in training and new medical equipment, and he was an outstanding fundraiser. He built the wing we're sitting in now. Dominion soon came to be known as the place to go if you wanted good care.

"Jim also decided we needed to be at the forefront of the transition to electronic medical records, so two years ago he brought in a young IT director, Barry Johnson, to lead that effort. That project is taking longer than expected, but we'll get there. Jim also believed strongly that diversity in the workplace would strengthen Dominion. Ryan Albert, our medical director, is African American and Julie Martinez, our vice president for marketing, is Hispanic."

Charlie noted that both Tom and Lee were taking notes. "They're actually listening," he thought, "or at least they're doing a pretty good imitation."

"What do you know about Jim's leadership style?" Tom asked, looking at Charlie over his reading glasses.

"Jim made it look effortless," Charlie replied. "I have the impression that he was a canny businessman who led his team and his board by not getting too far ahead of them. He built programs incrementally and supported his staff as they worked to put them in place. People are continually telling me what a wonderful man he was, that he was appreciative and generous. They tell me the executive team could turn to him for direction and that he had a knack for providing it. In the final analysis, the vision came from Jim, all the key decision making took place in Jim's office, and people looked to him to make those decisions.

"So Dominion today is really the reflection of one man's vision," Lee observed.

"To a large measure, it still is," Charlie said, instinctively looking around the office. "But the problem is, that man's gone. About a year ago, Jim was diagnosed with stage-three lung cancer—He had been a smoker—and started radiation and chemo right away."

"Seems like he would have been a tough act to follow," Tom observed.

"As it turned out, he was," said Charlie. "There was no succession plan. The board asked Bob to step in immediately while it engaged in a national search. I took over just about a year after Jim left."

There was a pause as Tom looked at his notes. "How did Bob work out?" Tom asked.

Tom and Lee could tell that Charlie was choosing his words carefully. "Bob is clearly very committed to the hospital and has been invaluable to me. He's worked here for more than 20 years and has a reputation for burning the midnight oil. He's told me Jim did not hold people fully accountable, and I got the feeling that it was a source of some tension between them. I think Bob, along with our CFO, Henry, were the two who worked behind the scenes to implement Jim's ideas.

"Sounds like the three of them together made a relatively effective leadership team," Tom said.

"They were," Charlie said thoughtfully. "Bob knows he doesn't have Jim's genial personality, but I don't think he thought it mattered when he took over as interim CEO. His approach was to immediately establish a number of fairly rigorous goals and hold people strictly accountable for reaching them. There wasn't much recognition if they did—it was what he expected of them—but there were penalties if they fell short. It's not exactly how I would have pulled a team together, either on the executive level or throughout the organization."

Charlie hesitated and then continued. "I think Jim and Bob, each in his own way, contributed to what I see are people problems that are undermining the performance at the hospital. I mentioned the infighting on the executive team and the troubling uptick in the turnover rate. Our exit interviews are taking on a negative tone. And we have to deal with the medical issue I referred to a while back. We have a serious MRSA outbreak that is cause for real concern, and the more I look into it, the more I see it's also a people issue. We know what we need to do to contain MRSA, but all I can tell you is that we're not doing it.

"I used to run track in high school, and I can see that as an organization, despite real individual skill and talent, we're dropping the baton all too often. And when I called an emergency meeting to discuss it, my normally friendly and polite executive team started blaming each other, instead of pulling together to deal with the problem."

Lee, who had been quiet for a while, leaned forward and asked, "So where does that leave you?"

"That's a good question," Charlie replied. "It feels like my leadership team wants me to be like Jim, wants me to give them direction. They seem to want approval from me—You should have seen them at the last management meeting when I summed up the MRSA situation—but at the same time, they also want to be left alone. It's a little odd, and it doesn't seem logical. Anyway, I'm not Jim. Even though his approach worked for 20 years, I think our management style now needs to be more collaborative."

Charlie hesitated for a second and then went on. "And I'm not Bob either. I agree with Bob that the need for accountability and commitment is important, but I don't think that's the whole issue here. The people I talk to on the executive team and throughout the hospital are very committed. I have a stack of proposals on my desk from different departments asking for resources. I've read them through, and there's a lot of hard work, passion, and vision there, but not an ounce of collaboration. I'm just not sure how to get people on the same page."

Producing a Healthy, High-Performance Organization

No one said anything, while Tom and Lee considered what Charlie had just told them. "Look, Charlie," said Lee. "We have a vision of a healthy workplace where the people side is optimized. A healthy workplace is where people are enthusiastic about their jobs and buy into the mission of the organization. It's where they are thinking of the whole enterprise when they deal with each other and their customers. It's where they find their job to be a rich and meaningful endeavor. They care for the larger organization and, in turn, the organization values them.

"One of our colleagues, John Pickering, calls this a *high-performance organization,* one that requires a very modern notion of the work environment. Instead of the old top-down management style that Jim and Bob practiced, we think in terms of creating a *networked talent model,* where people are interconnected. In these organizations every individual is involved in creating and carrying out the larger mission."

"If I understand what you are saying," Charlie said, "the networked talent model is what we need here, because folks are so interrelated in their jobs; the docs need to work with the nurses and the administrative staff and so on. Our ability to place the patient at the center of care is clearly dependent on everyone working together, which also means it can also be undermined by anyone."

Charlie made his decision. "Look, I like what I've been hearing, and I would like to engage you two, but let's be clear. I want to be part of the process. I don't want to be a bystander."

"If that's your preference, it's ours, too," said Tom, "and I'm not trying to be diplomatic."

"There's little chance of that," said Lee with a grin, looking at Tom. "But it just makes sense. There are three interrelated things we'll do: conduct an assessment of your staff culture, share the framework we developed that illuminates how people function in organizations, and help you develop an intervention plan for improving the people side of your business. How this process works in practice varies from client to client. We don't come in with standardized questionnaires and tests. We don't use off-the-shelf interventions. And we know that every organization is different and tailor our process accordingly."

"How about this?" Tom suggested. "Much of assessment is observation. Normally, we would do the observation together, but why don't you take the lead for now? You could continue to make your rounds of the hospital talking to people—gathering information and observing—and we could meet every week or so to talk over what you learn. This approach will ensure that we connect our work with your vision of the hospital and what you see going on. At each meeting, we'll discuss one of the six principles that we feel provide a framework for the people side of business, and at the end of our meeting, we'll introduce you to the next principle, so you can make it the focus of your next round of observations."

"That sounds good to me," Charlie said, "Why don't you put together a formal proposal and get it to me this week? Sally Heally, my vice president for human resources, gave me a ballpark figure for your costs. If there are no surprises we're on."

"We'll do that," Lee said. "But we're here now, and we'd be happy to talk to you about the first principle, simply stated as,

The brain works from the bottom up. It provides the foundation for the rest, and would be a good one to go over before you begin your assessment."

Charlie looked at his watch and stood up. "It's getting to be lunch time. What do you say we adjourn to The Nook and get lunch, and you can tell me about it there?"

Tom and Lee looked at each other. "Sounds like a plan," Lee said. "Lead on."

The Brain Works from the Bottom Up

A short while later, they were at The Nook, settling into a booth in the back. If the place had been quiet, you probably could have heard the waitstaff cracking their gum—but at noon, the restaurant was jammed and the racket made for privacy. The Nook was cheap, the food decent, and the service fast.

After they had studied their menus, Charlie looked at Tom and Lee and said, "For the record, I think working on the assessment and framework together is a good thing. My medical training really drove home the point that you don't intervene until you have a good idea of what's going on."

"I think our framework will help," Tom said. "Understand the six principles, act with them in mind, and you'll be able to develop a high-performance organization and move the hospital to the next level. The thing to remember—and it's what we'll be talking about over lunch—is that these principles are not arbitrary. They have their roots in the way our brains work. That's where they get their power."

The Third Domain of Organizational Excellence

After the waitress took their order, Tom nodded at Lee. "Lee is really fascinated by the evolutionary origins of behavior, so he'll take the lead explaining our first principle."

Charlie looked expectantly at Lee. "Here's the elevator speech," Lee said straightening his tie. "The fundamental idea behind our approach is that human behavior is a function of the brain's design, shaped by evolution over hundreds of thousands of years. From our point of view, it's critical to remember that primitive functions—involuntary physiological responses and emotions—always take precedence over higher-order rational processes. Sure, the ability to think rationally gives us a competitive edge, as a species and as individuals, but we wouldn't be around at all if we weren't hard-wired to survive in an environment that, for most of human history, has been rugged and dangerous. Physiological responses and emotions trump rational thought every time."

"When it comes down to it, everyone recognizes that rationality is not the whole picture," added Tom. "Mr. Spock is a Vulcan, not a human being, precisely because he's utterly logical and emotionless."

"Expecting people to come to work and act like rational, problem-solving Vulcans is wishful thinking," Lee went on. "People couldn't shed their physiological responses and emotions if they wanted to, because they are built in. So, as a manager, you have to work with the entire human organism as designed and then build systems compatible with that design. From what you've said about Bob, I think this is where he goes wrong."

Charlie thought about that for a few seconds. "That could be," he said. "Bob expects people to act logically, and seems baffled when they don't."

"That's probably right," said Lee. "And in the process he's missing a key component that can contribute to the success of an organization: people's emotions and instinctive reactions. In fact, passion is critical to an organization's future. As you've described Dominion, one of the qualities that comes through loud and clear is the staff's passionate commitment to helping patients. Align that passion with the goals of the organization, and you'll have a powerful engine for success.

"The phrase we use is, *The brain works from the bottom up.* We know you covered brain structure in medical school, but in business, the behavioral consequences of that structure are critical. The bottom of the brain, the brainstem, keeps basic functions operating, like respiration and heartbeat. It will preempt all other brain functions to keep a person alive. Let's say you're out on the savannah hunting and gathering, and you run into a saber-tooth tiger doing the same thing. You don't stop and think, 'Gee, there's a hungry-looking saber-tooth tiger. I wonder if there's any evasive action I can take?' Instead, your brain stem orders a load of adrenaline pumped into your blood, and you head for the hills."

Tom took up the thread, "When the brainstem registers distress, it's like being in a building when the fire alarm goes off. All work stops and everyone instinctively runs for the doors."

"And it's not just life-or-death situations that activate the brainstem," Lee continued. "Any kind of stress in the environment—hostile coworkers, sexual harassment, even second-hand smoke—can lead the brainstem to activate physiological responses that make it hard to think clearly. Most people think of programs and policies that discourage workplace violence and discrimination as a matter of equity or a way of reducing corporate liability, which are all true, but if you are trying to create an environment where people do their best thinking, those policies are essential."

The waitress arrived with their lunch. Charlie had a grilled cheese and tomato, Tom a BLT, and Lee, who was watching his weight, the salad plate. They were all quiet for a few minutes as they settled in to their food. Charlie was thinking about what Lee and Tom had been saying. "I can see your point about the brainstem taking precedence over rational process, but, by and large, basic survival is not an issue for my employees," he said. "At least not most days."

"That's good," said Lee. "But the fundamental point I'm making is not that your staff is in any danger of being attacked by saber-tooth tigers, but simply that evolutionary pressures have determined the way we're wired. I think you'll see my point when we look at the next level, the mid-brain, which is the seat of human emotions. The mid-brain influences our behavior constantly, shaping our decisions and influencing our view of the world whether we are conscious of it or not. Like the brainstem, the mid-brain also has the capacity to preempt rational thought."

Lee finished his forkful of cottage cheese and went on. "Here, too, we are dealing with evolutionary pressures. Our emotional responses—the desire to love and be loved, to belong to a community, to regard strangers suspiciously—not only boost the odds of our survival, but increase the likelihood that we'll succeed in passing our genes on to the next generation. These emotional drives are part of the hard-wiring that we all share, although the culture and conventions of everyday life tend to mask them. You mentioned that your normally well-mannered executive team got into a turf war when you called them together to deal with MRSA. When people feel threatened, they react emotionally, not logically."

Lee pointed his fork at Charlie. "We're not making a judgment about people. Emotional reactions are not intrinsically good or bad, but they do preempt logic. The stronger the emotion, the more it influences logical process. As I've said, these emotions can be beneficial, both for the individual and the company."

Discussing Brain Function over Lunch

Tom had finished the first half of his sandwich, so he introduced the next point. "The topmost portion of the brain, the cortex, is the seat of rational processing," he said, tapping his forehead. "We don't want to underestimate the power of the cortex, but it is a fundamental truth that rational processing is just part of what goes on in our brains. And the cortex is definitely not in charge. As Lee said, the cortex only works well when the lower two levels aren't agitated or agitating.

"People typically assume that the cortex, or thinking part of the brain, controls behavior and emotion. In fact, Charlie, the lower two parts of the brain stimulate thoughts, feelings, and behavior without reference to higher cortical functions. These lower two parts process information more quickly than the rational brain centers and initiate action on their own.

The Third Domain of Organizational Excellence

Fundamentally, managers and leaders need to understand that it's wrong to assume that people can act in a purely rational way. Systems for managing humans must take into account the design of the human brain much like software applications must be compatible with a computer's operating system."

Charlie paused with his sandwich in his hand. "You sure aren't optimistic about people," he remarked.

"On the contrary," Tom replied, as he finished off the rest of his BLT. "We think people can do great things, together and as individuals, but you have to accept them as they are. Only by starting with a more comprehensive, inclusive view of human behavior can you influence it. Human interactions are always a blend of instinct, emotion, and rationality.

Managers Are Not Therapists But Deal with Emotions

"That's why we think it is actually counterproductive for managers to tell their employees to leave their emotions at home," he continued. "In practice, that usually means if employees have had a fight with their spouse or if they're worried about making the next mortgage payment, we don't want to hear about it. On the other hand, we're happy to congratulate them when their children get engaged or they lower their handicap."

"But I don't have time to have a therapy session with every employee who's had a bad day," Charlie objected. He had finished his sandwich and was looking skeptically at Tom.

"That's not what we're trying to say," Tom replied, pushing away his plate. "You're not responsible for what happens outside the workplace, and you're not a therapist. No manager is. All you have to do is take a moment to acknowledge your employees' feelings and show that you are genuinely concerned. If you ignore the emotions your employees *bring to* work, you are going to have a hard time identifying the emotions *generated at* work and addressing them in a way that aligns them with Dominion's goals."

"All right, that makes sense," Charlie said after a pause. "So how would that play out in practice?

"Let's say an employee is depressed about something at home," Lee began. "By lending the employee a sympathetic ear, you at the very least encourage that employee's emotional connection to the company. It's not your responsibility to solve the underlying issues.

"When it comes to the emotions generated in the work environment, it's a different matter, because there you have the responsibility to think about emotions strategically and look at underlying causes. For example, when Jim got sick and abruptly left after leading the hospital for almost 20 years, it had to be a powerful emotional shock for the leadership team and for everyone else working at Dominion. They needed the opportunity to come together and express their worries about him and their anxieties about the future of Dominion.

"Instead, Bob redoubled the pressure on everyone and set higher goals. By ignoring their emotions, Bob missed an opportunity to use the power of their emotions to bring the team together. Even worse, he created negative feelings that are as destructive to your system as MRSA."

"This ties in with what Daniel Goleman says in *Emotional Intelligence*," said Charlie, referring to one of his favorite volumes on his bookshelf.

"That's a good point," Lee said. "I know you don't have a lot of time for reading, but you might want to go back and take another look at his ideas about connecting people's emotional reactions to different triggers. You can apply these insights to Dominion."

"I'll make the time to do that," Charlie said. "But the problem for me is the mix of personalities I have to deal with. You should have heard Barry, my IT guy; and Julie, my marketing VP, go after each other at the emergency executive team meeting I called two weeks ago. People respond to the same situation in very different ways. Creating that high-performance organization we were talking about with people like that is not going to be easy."

"You're right there," Tom said as the waitress brought the check. "And that brings us to our last point. We all share similar emotional responses, but they're embedded in our individual personalities: the combination of our genes, brain structure, and formative experiences. Our personality shapes the way we interpret information and express emotions, and personality is damned hard to change. We know, because we work day in and day out in our clinical offices helping people attempt to change, and these are people who come asking and wanting to change. We don't recommend trying to change people in the work environment.

"And while we're talking about books, I'll remind you that in another book on your bookshelf, *First, Break All the Rules,* the researchers from Gallup found that managers in successful companies don't try to change people's personalities. They don't waste time trying to put in what was left out. They try to draw out what was left in. In any case, hang on to that thought. We'll go back to personality when we get to our last principle."

They split the check and stood up. "So what's next?" Charlie asked as they filed out past the cash register. "I understand that the brain works from the bottom up; that behavior is a blend of instinct, emotion, and rationality; and that managers who fail to consider emotions do so at their own peril. What do I have to do so that Dominion benefits from people's emotions?

"Funny you should ask," said Lee. "Your question leads right to our second principle: *People are most productive in an emotionally safe and supportive environment.*"

"That was pretty neat, wasn't it?" Charlie said, grinning.

"Sure, but it points out that there's a logic to the way people act, a logic that's highlighted by our principles," responded Lee. "Look, let's meet every week or so for the time being. In the meantime, focus your assessment efforts on finding out if your people feel cared for. You can watch, observe, and ask questions—Don't worry about being too direct—then we can get together and talk over what you've discovered. As things begin to gather steam, we will find our rhythm, and Tom and I will get more involved in the assessment process. By the time we're finished rolling out the principles, we'll all have enough information to begin putting together an effective intervention. We'll spell out the details in our proposal."

Charlie drove them back to the Dominion lot and parked next to Lee's Ford. The three shook hands. "I'm curious about what I'm going to find out," Charlie said. "This is a bit of an adventure."

"Try to enjoy it," Lee advised. "Anything you discover—even the unpleasant surprises—can help you get Dominion back on track. And if you have any questions, don't hesitate to touch base."

As he walked through the hospital entrance, Charlie thought about how straightforward this whole process seemed to be. Tom and Lee certainly took a low-key approach, with no 360-degree evaluations, no Meyers-Briggs inventories. They wanted to find out what was going on at Dominion, and they were helping him see it with new eyes. "This could be very interesting," he said to himself as he looked at his watch and headed to his one o'clock meeting.

Principle 1: The design of the brain determines human behavior

1. The design of the brain determines human behavior, giving primitive functions precedence over higher-order rational processes. The brain consists of three major regions: the brainstem, the mid-brain, and the cortex. The brainstem controls physiological functions such as heartbeat, respiration, and fight-or-flight mechanisms. The mid-brain is the source of emotional processes. Conscious rational processing emerges in the top layer, the cerebral cortex. Primitive functions—physiologic regulation and emotions—have precedence over rational processes. The lower parts must be satisfied for the higher cortical processes to operate freely and effectively.

2. Systems for managing humans must function within the design parameters of the human brain. Human interactions are a blend of instinct, emotion, and rationality. Whether people are aware of the emotional component of their behavior at work or not, it is impossible for them to leave their emotions at home. Accordingly, only by starting with a more comprehensive, inclusive view of human behavior can managers recognize typical emotional responses and manage them in the best interests of the company.

3. Changing personality is very difficult and not a manager's responsibility. We all share similar emotional responses, but they are embedded in our individual personalities: the combination of our brain structure, inherited genes, and formative experiences. Personality shapes the way we interpret information and express emotions.

CHAPTER 2

PEOPLE ARE MOST PRODUCTIVE IN AN EMOTIONALLY SAFE AND SUPPORTIVE ENVIRONMENT

Charlie was standing in front of the visitors elevator on the third floor. It was Wednesday morning, two days after his lunch with Tom and Lee. He glanced briefly at the indicator counting down from the top floor, but his mind was elsewhere, mulling over the conversations he had been having with members of the staff. He had anticipated that asking employees about their feelings was going to cause some raised eyebrows, but he had underestimated the extent of their resistance. He had tried to weave his questions naturally into the conversations, but the tactic hadn't seemed to help. Certainly, people were polite and pleasant, but they were almost uniformly noncommittal and uninformative.

"It's not as if I'm a stranger," Charlie thought. Since he had taken over as CEO three months ago, he had made it his practice to get to the hospital early, spending some time before business hours introducing himself to staff and asking people how they were doing. He had enjoyed getting to know the building and the distinct rhythms of the place. And, as Charlie had discovered, Jim had done an excellent job designing the new wing and renovating the original building. The individual wards and specialty units were spacious and well laid out. Patient rooms were bright and attractive, and the nurses stations were centrally located and carefully organized. Charlie was becoming attached to the place; there was no doubt about it.

For three months now, Charlie had been urging the people he met on his early-morning rounds to e-mail him if they had an idea for improving the hospital, but his inbox was not exactly overflowing with suggestions. He was disappointed, but Charlie had supposed it would take some time before staff felt comfortable opening up to a new CEO. Now he began to think that bashfulness was not the problem. Waiting for the elevator, the thought struck him that the lack of response in both cases pointed in the same direction. "If people felt safe, secure, cared for, there would be no hesitation in telling me so," he thought as the elevator chimed and the door opened. "But what's holding them back?"

Charlie reflexively blocked the door from closing until the last visitor had entered and then got in himself. The only direct response he had received in two hours of walking his rounds on two separate days was from a highly regarded clinical nurse specialist he had encountered hovering over a computer terminal in pediatrics. When, after a few questions, he got around to asking her if the hospital made her feel cared for, she was blunt. "If someone cared about me," she said, "they would have fixed this damned computer system a long time ago. To process these blood profiles, I have to reenter all of the patient data, right down to address and telephone number, before the system accepts the profile. I understand the need for patient safety, but there has to be a better way. I'm doing my best to take care of my patients, and I'm wasting my time."

When Charlie asked her if she had talked to the IT department about it, she snorted, "Sure I have, several times, but nothing has ever come of it. No one seems to be listening." Charlie let her get back to the task and made a mental note for Barry to send one of his programmers down to talk to her and come up with a fix.

When the door opened at the lobby level, Charlie headed back to his office. As he walked down the corridor, he continued trying to draw some conclusions from the employee responses. "Okay, I know people don't feel cared for," he thought to himself, "and one reason could be that they feel no one pays attention to them. But there has to be more I could find out. Maybe it's the way I'm approaching things." Instead of beating around the bush and weaving the question into the conversation, he resolved to cut to the chase the next morning and keep it simple. He also thought he would check in with staff in the surgery and oncology departments on Friday. Those were two of his best units; surely they would feel cared for. He decided to have his assistant make appointments for him to talk with the heads of those departments so that he could get the complete picture. They included Ryan Albert in oncology, who also served on his executive team as the hospital's medical director.

Thursday's direct conversations turned out to shed a little more light on his questions, although the responses were evasive in their own way. People told him a lot about how safe and supported they felt when Jim was CEO. In fact, just about everyone he talked to felt that Jim was there for them, that he was attentive and kind, and that he trusted them to focus on their work and give it their best. They really missed him.

Charlie realized, though, that there were two significant omissions to their responses: they didn't talk about Bob and they never mentioned him. Not a single person talked about how he or she felt right now. That wasn't good.

On Friday, Charlie concentrated on interviewing the surgery and oncology staff. The pride that members of both groups took in their work impressed him. From his conversations, he found that they placed a premium on professionalism, compassionate care, and working well together. When Charlie asked if they felt that the hospital cared for them, however, they tended to restate the question in terms of their own units. They felt valued as a contributing member of the surgery team or as a player on the oncology team, but not as part of the overall Dominion staff.

A Pointed Conversation with the Chief of Surgery

After his conversations with staff, Charlie headed to the office of Dr. Lou Perrott, the chief of surgery. Lou was a balding, studious-looking doctor, serious about his job. Regarded as one of Jim's early successful finds, he'd been with Dominion for 18 years. He was thoughtful, competent, and deliberate in manner. More easygoing than many surgeons, he got along well with his staff and patients.

Charlie had been to Lou's office before and knew what to expect. Attached to the wall behind Lou's desk, alongside a set of sailing pictures, was an eight-foot harpoon that Lou's wife had discovered in an antique shop in New Bedford. Lou had been an English major in college, as the story went, with a fondness for *Moby Dick*, and thought it a marvelous gift. When asked, he said that the harpoon contrasted nicely with the equally sharp, though more delicate, scalpels he used on a daily basis. It never occurred to him that the huge weapon hanging on the wall behind him might make some visitors uncomfortable.

Taking his seat while staring at the harpoon above Lou, Charlie felt compelled to get right down to business. "I've been trying to figure out if the MRSA outbreak and other issues we're dealing with hospital-wide—the rising turnover rate, for instance—reflect something that's missing in the way we deal with staff," he said. "I guess another way to look at this is whether you think the staff feels cared for."

The chief appeared perplexed by the question, "I guess I do," he said tentatively. "Of course we all care about the staff, but the bottom line in surgery is patient outcomes. Fundamentally, I assume that all our staff knows that we want them to do everything possible to give our patients the best possible treatment."

"I think you're right," said Charlie. "I was just interested in whether we did anything specific for individual staff members to show that we care about their efforts, which would demonstrate that Dominion is a caring environment."

"I'm not sure it matters what they think about Dominion. What motivates me—and my staff—is providing the best medical care possible. That's its own reward, isn't it? We are all here because we find satisfaction in helping people. My job is to give my people—especially my surgeons—the tools to do just that."

Charlie then headed over to oncology for his meeting with Ryan. On the way, Charlie thought about what his surgery chief had told him. Of course, he was right: their sense of mission was what drove the staff, but on the other hand, that didn't mean that they wouldn't benefit from being recognized for their efforts.

The Medical Director's Perspective

Charlie had gotten to know Ryan pretty well as the hospital's medical director. Now he would be talking to him as the head of oncology, and he wondered if that would make a difference.

"You want me to tell you whether staff feels cared for and whether we've created a caring environment at Dominion?" Ryan asked.

"That's right," Charlie replied.

"They're really two separate questions, but they are related," Ryan replied. "I'll start with the second and move back to the first. Here's some history. Stop me if you already know it. When I arrived at Dominion five years ago, Jim gave me a mandate to create a topnotch cancer center, and gave me carte blanche to do it. I knew from my experience and from the research that creating a caring environment—encouraging staff to reach out to patients—has a significant impact on outcomes. It's also the compassionate thing to do. We sent our staff to seminars so that they could bring the latest thinking on patient care back to Dominion, and we found funds to support their initiatives when we thought they would help.

"So far so good, until Jim got sick. When Bob took over, he sent out a strong message that each department was a cost center and had to watch its bottom line. That's how we had been operating, but it soon became apparent that what Jim considered a cost center and what Bob considered a cost center were two different things. Henry started to bounce our budgets back to us, redlining many of the initiatives that made this place more nurturing, for staff as well as patients. I met with Bob and Henry, but got nowhere. They thought our efforts to build supportive relationships with patients were so much fluff. And they severely restricted training for everyone but physicians, so we started to make cuts. As soon as we did that, the atmosphere in this place began to change. And it was not just the patients who suffered; I think staff felt the cuts were a rebuke—and to be totally frank so did I. I mean, Bob and Henry know next to nothing about cancer care, and they're telling us what to do!"

Charlie saw that Ryan was getting angry even thinking about the experience. "They sent the message that what counts at Dominion is not the patient and is certainly not the staff. It's just the bottom line.

"I remain here despite my frustration with the situation because I am committed to my staff, the patients, and this community. And I stay because I think you're interested in changing the culture of this place and readjusting our priorities."

Ryan left his underlying message unspoken, knowing that Charlie would pick up on it—and he did. Charlie knew that an experienced physician and talented administrator, trained at some of the best medical schools in country, with a résumé studded with honors, and an African American to boot, could go anywhere. If things didn't change soon, Ryan was telling him, he would start looking for another position. Ryan would be tough to replace. Charlie also knew that Dominion could ill afford to lose one of its few black leaders.

"It means a lot to me that you'll stick with Dominion," said Charlie. "I'd like to make Dominion a caring place once again, but it may take time for our leadership team to get on board. I don't want to just dictate change from the top. That's not the way to make it stick. If you can find ways to help me as we move forward, I would greatly appreciate it."

Ryan nodded, and Charlie looked at his watch. "It's time for our executive team meeting," he said. "Let's walk over together. I'm interested in hearing your report about MRSA."

Charlie Challenges the Executive Team

As Charlie entered the conference room and took his place at the head of the table, it struck him once again, as it had so many times, that the men positioned themselves on one side of the table and the women on the other. Bob sat to his right, followed by Henry and Barry in that order—although Barry

42

hadn't made an appearance yet. The three women, Debbie, Julie, and Sally, invariably sat to his left, though they occasionally changed places. The COO, CFO, and vice president for IT sat to the right. The director of nursing, vice president for marketing, and the vice president for human resources sat at his left. Ryan always took the chair opposite him. Clearly Dominion had a long way to go to become the high-performance, interconnected organization that Tom and Lee were talking about.

There was plenty on the agenda. As CFO, Henry Powell was in the midst of a report about Medicare reimbursement trends when Barry arrived and slumped into his seat. Charlie observed that Barry didn't seem to be in any hurry to get to the meeting or apologetic about being late. When Henry finished, the team turned its attention to MRSA. Each manager had responded to Ryan and Sally's memo on infection control procedures and reported that they had reviewed the protocols with their teams and urged them to intensify their efforts. Patients suffering from MRSA were being well cared for—and thankfully none of their cases so far was serious. And the hospital-wide MRSA task force that Ryan and Sally had established as part of their MRSA plan had held two meetings. The task force had already identified a number of places where better coordination between the different services could help.

The results were encouraging, but, Charlie knew, it was far too early to know if the hospital was making progress. It would be another week and a half yet before they would get the next set of figures from the Quality Assurance Committee, and it would take a few months for them to know with any certainty whether they had the outbreak under control. Charlie complimented everyone and then got to an item of business he had left off the agenda.

"As I've mentioned to some of you, I am convinced that this MRSA outbreak is just one symptom of a larger people problem in the hospital, one that includes higher-than-normal turnover rates and a number of smaller issues that I've discovered in talking with staff. I'm convinced we will have further outbreaks if we don't directly improve the people culture at Dominion, which is something I want the executive team to address as a cohesive unit. I have engaged two consultants, Lee Hersch and Tom DeMaio, to help us. They'll be sitting in on our meetings as part of their effort to get to know us better, and I plan to take an active part in their initial assessment as well. So, in the last 15 minutes of the meeting, I would like to get your response to questions I've been asking staff. Do you think that our employees feel cared for? Do you think they feel like their supervisors care about them as people?"

There were quizzical looks from some around the table. No one wanted to be the first one to speak. "Well, we do have an employee-of-the-month parking spot," said Barry. Now there were chuckles and then another awkward pause.

Finally, Henry looked around and volunteered, "Of course we care for the staff. Who wouldn't think that?"

But Charlie pressed on, "Henry, it's not what *we* think that's ultimately important. It's what *they* think, so the question still stands: what do we do to make our staff feel valued, cared for, important?"

There was another silence. "I think we have bigger fish to fry than whether the staff feels appreciated," Bob finally said, not quite concealing his exasperation. "We have a dangerous outbreak on our hands. That's a serious quality control issue. Shouldn't we be focusing 100 percent on making sure we maintain a safe environment, never mind retaining our certification as a hospital? Sure, I'd like for people to feel cared for, but I think we need to keep our priorities straight and concentrate on performance issues."

Henry raised his hand. "I see where you're going with this, Charlie, but we can only worry about the soft stuff so much. Unless we protect the bottom line, no one has job security, and patients won't get care. For so many years, especially while Jim was CEO, we operated close to the bone. Our margins were barely adequate to finance the equipment and facilities renovation we've undertaken. Things are better now, but we're still not out of the woods.

"For my part, I think we should focus on shooting for margins greater than 5 percent, while continuing to set aside funds to reinvest in technology and modernization. Without that, we won't be able to remain competitive, and unless we're competitive, it's not going to matter whether the staff feels appreciated. While I'm not against being caring, I'm not sure we can afford the effort unless we are really on top of our financial game."

Charlie wasn't surprised by the position staked out by Bob and Henry—It was the mirror image of what he heard from the staff—but it was dismaying nonetheless. He had his work cut out for him.

Across the table, Ryan was being noncommittal. He was taking a wait-and-see attitude. Charlie looked to his left. On the women's side of the table, Julie Martinez looked like she was making a decision. "Personnel isn't my field," she finally said, "but how the staff feels plays a big role in marketing. We all know that the most effective form of marketing is word of mouth. Will our customers—or in this case our patients—recommend Dominion to their friends and neighbors? Our surveys have shown that patients feel the quality of medical care we offer continues to be very good. We haven't evaluated the patient experience, however, in more than two years. I'm not sure how people feel about how we've treated them here.

"But no one comes to a hospital to enjoy themselves," Henry said, looking puzzled.

"True, but you have to admit that it does make a difference—both to their outcomes and to our bottom line—if they are treated well while they are here. Other hospitals out there compete with us for patients. And this is not just the nursing staff's responsibility," Julie said, nodding at Debbie Smith, the director of nursing. "Dozens of people, from the physicians to housekeeping to billing, interact with each patient. It only takes one bad encounter to sabotage a positive experience."

"What does this have to do with our staff feeling cared for?" Bob asked. "I don't see the connection."

"I do," Julie replied. "I am convinced that there is a link between patience experience and whether our staff feels cared for. Our goal here has always been to provide high-quality care—but there are many ways to do that. We are under no obligation to install a television in every room or a comfortable seat for family members, but we do anyway, because we want to make our patients' experience here as comfortable as possible. How well our staff treats them helps determine this experience. If we do the kinds of things that make our staff feel cared for, they'll do the kinds of things that make our patients feel cared for. Considered just from a marketing point of view, we've never given the issue of whether our staff feels cared for the degree of attention it deserves."

Charlie noticed that even though Julie recognized that the whole hospital had to band together to solve the people problem, she was really making the case from a marketing perspective.

Sitting next to Julie, Sally Healy was listening attentively. She appreciated Julie stepping up. After all, human resources was Sally's department, not Julie's. She also appreciated Julie's effort to deflect criticism from Debbie, who seemed especially sensitive to it. In any case, Sally wasn't going to leave Julie hanging out on a limb.

"I agree with Julie, and think it's fair to say that we haven't focused on whether the staff feels valued," she said. "We offer a number of policies and programs, like child care and compassionate leave, that go beyond the norms in our industry. We offer them because we think it's the right thing to do. I'm not sure we have considered whether those are policies and programs that our staff wants. In a survey that had been conducted right before I came on board two years ago, our staff reported a reasonable level of job satisfaction, nothing special, but still reasonable. As you know, however, there has been an increased amount of turnover in the last six to nine months. There's no hard data to explain this, Charlie, but I suspect you're on to something."

The two sides of the table had spoken, and there was no apparent path to reconciliation. Charlie looked expectantly at Ryan to see if he might add anything. After all, Ryan had stressed the importance of supporting staff and making patients feel emotionally cared for and had expressed his anger at the budget cutbacks that made it hard for him to do just that. But Ryan was now playing his cards close to his chest. Charlie sighed. He'd hoped that Ryan would be more forthcoming in the team meeting. He looked at his watch. "Well, I promised you'd get out of here at ten, and I'm going to let you go, but we will be coming back to this.

"And Barry, I need to talk to you for a second about a computer issue I noticed in pediatrics."

Seeking Diverse Perspectives

On Monday morning, Charlie scheduled back-to-back meetings with Julie and Sally, marketing and human resources, for later that afternoon. He wanted to follow up on their remarks from the executive team meeting. Charlie had sensed the resentment coming from the left side of the table and understood that the women on his executive team felt that Bob and Henry were holding them back. At least Julie and Sally were now starting to speak up—and he wanted to know more. The nursing director, Debbie, still puzzled him, but Charlie thought he would wait to talk to her until he got a better idea of what was bothering her.

"Charlie, the answer to your question about marketing's role at Dominion is to follow the money," Julie said, after Charlie explained why he had called her in. "We put our money into our buildings, our technology, and our cutting-edge procedures. The truth of the matter is that marketing here is just an afterthought." The angry edge in Julie's voice took Charlie by surprise.

"Jim was proud of our status as a regional hospital and our ability to compete with the large tertiary-care facilities, but the market research on the value of personalized care was not convincing to him. On top of that, he didn't buy the link between the staff feeling cared about and a positive patient experience. In fact, I had the feeling that he dismissed the idea out of hand. It just wasn't the way he thought about things."

Julie pointed at the copy of *Good to Great* that Charlie kept on his bookshelf. "You know what Jim Collins says about how important it is for companies to pay attention to customer preferences. Collins compares Kroger, which adapted its stores to the kind of shopping experience its customers were looking for, with A&P, which kept insisting on maintaining the traditional grocery store environment that had served it so well for a hundred years. Kroger grew and A&P didn't.

"My problem is that I have a Kroger's mindset, but I'm working for A&P," Julie said with half a smile. "Jim really didn't think much of marketing. For him, putting a few ads in the paper and maybe a radio spot or two every few months was enough. Jim believed that if you do good work, people will show up at your door. And he believed in treating the staff well, but he didn't think that treating staff well would, over the long run, lead to consistently higher utilization, and there was nothing I could do to convince him.

The Third Domain of Organizational Excellence

"I ran up against a similar wall with Bob, though Bob's response was different from Jim's. Bob likes things to be measurable— That's just the way he is—and that's not always possible with marketing. If you can't measure, you can't hold people account-able, and Bob really is a stickler for accountability. But I think there's another issue operating there as well. Bob doesn't seem comfortable with emotions, or maybe it's more accurate to say he doesn't seem to acknowledge them. Whether we like it or not, people have an emotional response to the care they receive here, and if we can make it a positive response, then more people will stay here. And if we treat our staff well in ways that matter to them, they'll treat our patients well in ways that they care about."

All of a sudden, Julie felt herself run out of steam. She had believed that Charlie would know what she was talking about, but now, when he didn't seem to react, she thought to herself, "Well, what do I really know about him?" Julie was a bit sur-prised at her hesitancy, because she generally thought of her-self as a no-nonsense person. The oldest child—and a girl— in a traditional Hispanic household, she was determined, as a first-generation American, to create a life of her own. Her parents were tremendously proud of her, but recently Julie had been wondering if she was indeed as successful as they believed. Launching herself into the world from a poor neigh-borhood in Los Angeles seemed like child's play compared to finding her place in what she saw as the old boy network at Dominion. The fact of the matter was that she didn't know how much longer she could fight the same old battles.

For his part, Charlie was stunned. He had a sense of what it took for Julie to finally talk frankly about her experiences at

Dominion. In a way, he had spent his entire last week trying to find someone with the courage to be honest with him, and he was grateful. "Julie, all I can say right now is that I hear you, loud and clear," said Charlie slowly. "I agree with your assessment. I appreciate your honesty and hope very much that you will keep speaking your mind." Julie nodded tentatively.

"At the same time, I can't make these changes by myself and hope for them to stick without buy-in from the leadership team. That's only going to happen when the team shares a common vision and commitment. That's why I've asked Tom DeMaio and Lee Hersch to help us out. So I'm asking you to bear with me." Julie nodded again.

"Well," she thought to herself, "I should at least give this guy a chance."

Charlie had scheduled Julie and Sally back to back, and the two women exchanged a few words as they passed in Charlie's waiting room. Sally noticed that Julie looked a bit more relaxed than she had lately.

Charlie ushered Sally into his office, and they sat down around Charlie's conference table. Sally noticed that Charlie had been doing a little computer shopping. He had replaced Bob's old computer and metal table with a laptop that he kept on the corner of his desk. It somehow made the room look a bit more inviting.

"Sally, I want to begin by saying that I've been pleased with your leadership on the MRSA task force. You and Ryan have done an excellent job. Sally smiled.

"I've also been thinking about what you said at the executive team meeting on Friday," Charlie began. "I appreciated your backing me up on the importance of recognizing the people issues in the organization. Frankly, I would have been surprised if you hadn't. But I also was curious about why you think our employee satisfaction numbers were never better than national norms, even under Jim. What do you think was the issue?"

Sally considered Charlie's question for a second. "I worked with Jim for less than a year, so it's hard to tell exactly. Jim was a businessman and a good one, but he also wanted to do right by his employees—at least as he understood the phrase. Jim treated people nicely; there was a pleasant paternalistic feeling here, sort of a *Father Knows Best* atmosphere, and the staff generally liked it. Jim made sure we offered a pretty good benefits package. The staff certainly felt loyalty to Jim, but I'm not sure that translates into loyalty to Dominion, which is why the institutional scores were never as high as they could have been."

"And now?" Charlie asked.

"And now, Jim's gone, and the staff still feels a little lost. And Bob," she trailed off. "Bob doesn't really see the people issues. He believes that holding people accountable is the answer for any problem Dominion runs into. When he took over, his 100 percent emphasis on accountability hit us all like a bucket of ice water. Maybe we needed it, Charlie, but it created an environment of uncertainty and some fear. And it never seemed that there was any satisfying him; if you met his targets, he cranked them up higher. And there were never any rewards for a job well done, not even a pat on the back.

"In my view, we have to shift our approach and provide a genuinely supportive environment for the staff, or our turnover is just going to get worse. My sense is that our staff members don't express their dissatisfaction; they are reserved and polite until the day they walk."

Charlie thought about his conversations with the staff over the last week. "That's been my impression as well."

"The bottom line is that I'm worried about Dominion," Sally continued. "Let me be frank: my dad was an alcoholic, and I'm always on the lookout to solve problems before they have a chance to get out of hand, so maybe I'm overreacting, but I don't think so. I don't exactly know what needs to be done to get Dominion back on track, but I do know that we're going to have to pull together to make it happen. And at least on the executive team, we have a long way to go."

Charlie was silent for a moment. Sally was the only person he had talked to who was thinking in terms of Dominion—and the only one who understood that solving the people problem had to involve all of them.

"Sally, I appreciate your advice. All I can tell you is that I'm committed to developing a more supportive culture at Dominion, and I know it will take a team effort. I'm just not clear in my mind right now how I'm going to create a functioning executive team at Dominion. I'm hoping the consultants you recommended, Lee Hersch and Tom DeMaio, can help me out."

"I hope so, too," said Sally. "In any case, you can count on me."

The Third Domain of Organizational Excellence

After Charlie left, he thought more about the divide between the men and the women on his executive team. Julie and Sally seemed to appreciate that he listened to them. The men didn't seem to want to hear what he had to say. Getting the two groups to coalesce was going to be a challenge.

The Importance of an Emotionally Safe and Supportive Environment

The next day, Tuesday, Charlie met again with Tom and Lee to review his findings from his week of interviews and observations and to find out more about why they placed such a premium on creating a caring environment. As they settled around his conference table, Tom looked at him curiously and asked, "So, how did it go?"

Charlie smiled. "You know," he said, "I discovered a lot about Dominion. Some of it was stuff I think I already knew, but hadn't really focused on, if you know what I mean. I've been thinking about it, and you can divide my findings into the not-so-good and the good. I'm dividing them that way because, on the whole, I feel pretty optimistic about being able to turn Dominion around.

"Let's start with the not-so-good. I found that, by and large, people don't feel cared for at Dominion or even listened to— with the result that they themselves tend to be standoffish, suspicious, and I think a little resentful. I only had to go as far as my executive team to see that resentment in action. It's no wonder we have a MRSA outbreak and are having such a hard time pulling together to fight it.

"I also found out a little bit about why we're in the position we are today. Even under Jim, who treated people well, there was no sense that management needed to do anything special to make people feel appreciated and welcomed. Jim felt that doing good was its own reward, and Bob managed by holding people accountable without any corresponding sense that people needed some support. Bob thinks people can and should leave their emotions at home. Given what we discussed over lunch about emotions being hard-wired into our brains as a way to ensure our survival, and about emotions taking precedence over thought, it's not surprising that Bob's approach fell short.

"Okay, now for the good. I've found that people here are really dedicated to serving patients, to providing high-quality medical care, and they are really good about the technical aspects of their jobs. Their professionalism impressed me. At the same time, with some exceptions, they don't seem to go out of their way to reach out to their patients. I guess that's a mixture of good and not-so-good.

"Finally, there's the 100 percent good. I've found a number of people on the executive team who seem open to dealing with the people issues at Dominion. In fact, they have been eager to address these issues for some time, but have felt thwarted. They seem, to varying degrees, ready to help us move forward."

Tom and Lee were taking notes. "This sounds promising," said Tom, peering over his reading glasses. "Let's go through your observations day by day so we can get a clearer picture of what you've encountered so far."

The Third Domain of Organizational Excellence

After Charlie carefully described his week, the three of them sat back, considering. "Let me see if I can clarify a few things in my own mind," Lee said after a second. "From what you've said, it's apparent that making the staff feel highly valued has not been an intentional priority of Dominion's leadership."

"Correct," Charlie responded. "Jim made people feel good. That's what virtually everyone told me, but I don't think it was intentional or strategic. It was just his way with people. And Bob didn't have the habit, the insight, or the intention."

"So as far as you know, creating a supportive environment for staff has never been on the radar screen at this organization," Lee went on. "While the scores on the staff satisfaction survey conducted before Sally came on board were no more than middling, no one paid them much attention. Jim assumed that because he cared, the staff would feel cared for. Bob didn't track this issue and didn't know he was failing."

"I think that's right," Charlie said.

Lee nodded, and Charlie went on. "Now, I heard a lot from Julie and Sally about how making the staff members feel valued would increase the likelihood that they would, in turn, provide patients with a more caring experience, which would be good for our numbers. I think I get that. But I'm still not wholly clear about why making people feel cared for is going to help Dominion become a more productive place."

"That's a great question, said Lee, and it ties right into our second principle: *People are most productive in an emotionally safe and supportive environment*. This principle is a direct consequence of the evolutionary forces we discussed at lunch. The brain is wired for survival, so safety and security are paramount."

Personal Is Perceived as a Threat

Lee continued, "If people think their jobs are threatened, those primitive protective mechanisms take charge. They feel rejected and abandoned. They start making decisions to ensure their own job security, rather than focusing on the best interests of the company. They start acting defensively, blaming others, and being exceptionally careful. They are not creative or team-oriented. Sound familiar?"

"So that's what was going on during all those conversations," Charlie said looking puzzled. "That's so weird. I was just asking questions, not threatening their jobs."

"But that's not the point," Tom replied. "They don't really even see you, Charlie. They're responding to Bob's single-minded focus on accountability, a focus that you've inherited. From what you've told us, the message they got from Bob is that the organization will accept them only as long as they meet his standards. If they fall short, they face rejection. Twenty thousand years ago, this meant being cast out of the family cave. At Dominion, this could translate into a poor performance evaluation or a pink slip. It sounds to me like a logical cause for anxiety. People are likely to perceive you as a potential threat until you demonstrate otherwise."

"You're no doubt familiar with Abraham Maslow's hierarchy of needs," said Lee. "It's hard to get through college these days without hearing about it in some form."

"Psych 101. Professor Maas," Charlie said, "although the only thing I can remember about Maslow from his class is that I thought being self-actualized might improve my social life."

"Well, it's true that one of Maslow's points was that people have to satisfy their more primitive needs before they get to address their higher-order ones," Lee continued, "but he was mostly talking about safety and security. You can see that playing out at Dominion."

"The imperative to attach to other humans is incredibly powerful," Tom went on. "It starts at birth. Look at the way infants and children attach to their parents, how they look into their parents' eyes. At the same time, it's important to remember that attachment operates throughout life. We remain programmed to respond to threats to the attachments we've formed, and we do so whether these threats are real or perceived. The mere absence of clear signs of acceptance can create anxiety. No matter how secure a person seems to be, some part of them is keeping an eye out for warnings that they are in danger of rejection. So, if people don't feel cared for, or valued, or important, or loved, or whatever you want to call it by the organization, then they are less likely to feel safe and secure, to be attached to the mission, and to perform optimally."

Tom continued, "These are not learned behaviors, but rather hard-wired emotional reactions. And this is why we think it's just plain common sense that executives make an intentional effort to manage some of these basic emotional responses. Making people feel valued reduces stress, allows people to engage in the work at hand, and helps them commit to the mission of the organization. How can you complain about that?"

Charlie thought about Ryan Albert, his medical director. When they had met at the cancer center, Ryan had told him in so many words that Bob made him and his staff feel devalued and that if things didn't change, he was going to leave, essentially attach himself somewhere else where he would be appreciated. On the other hand, Sally's sense of attachment seemed more resilient. Even after several years of feeling ignored, the human resources vice president still seemed willing to stick with Dominion. She was ready to take a chance on his leadership.

"Just from what I've seen," Charlie said, thinking about Sally and Ryan and the rest of the executive team, "people react to these emotional triggers in different ways. What can I do about that?"

"Every employee brings to work an approach to attachment that was determined by their genes and by the degree to which they felt cared for and attached in their family," Tom responded.

"Their personality," said Charlie.

"That's right. And organizations can't change someone's personality, and they shouldn't even try. They have neither the expertise nor the responsibility. What they can do is maximize the degree to which people feel valued and connected in the work environment. When we get to our sixth principle, we'll talk more about how to manage diverse employees."

"But let's get back to Bob for a second," Charlie said. "Bob may be a by-the-books guy, but he doesn't have a mean bone in his body. And he is dedicated to the hospital. I think he would be genuinely shocked to find out that people feel threatened by him."

The Third Domain of Organizational Excellence

"That's probably true," said Lee. "Some people are poor judges of how other people perceive them. Think of Lou and his harpoon! Look, Bob sounds like he has been very dedicated to the hospital and to its mission, but ironically, by pursuing the issue *his way*, without regard to people's emotions, he provoked fear. Instead of the great performance he expected, he got mediocre results. And he chased off some of your best people and alienated others."

"In business school I had to write a paper about W. Edwards Deming," said Charlie, "the management consultant who transformed Japanese manufacturing in the 1950s and 1960s— Toyota, Sony, Panasonic. They all owe a debt to him. Anyway, he developed 14 principles for managers who wanted to boost the effectiveness of their organizations, and his eighth was 'Drive out fear, so that everyone may work effectively for the company.' I always thought that the fear issue was more about abusive, threatening bosses. But I'll bet it applies more often to well-meaning managers like Bob."

The Benefits of Caring

"I think you're right," Tom said. "And the most effective way we know to drive out fear is to make people feel cared for. When there aren't intentional efforts to have the staff feel valued, fear can easily creep in. Workers actually need specific people, like their manager or supervisor, to show caring for them at work.

"But caring for people is not just about driving out fear. When people feel cared for, when they are not worried about their survival or, these days, about whether they are going to lose their jobs, they can think clearly. Companies benefit. And if people feel genuinely attached, they're willing to take those kinds of creative and intellectual leaps that can make a company dramatically more successful. In an accepting culture, people take these sorts of risks because they don't fear rejection if they fail. That's another benefit. Finally, companies benefit when people are unafraid to express their opinions and challenge accepted wisdom. Banishing fear is a prerequisite for innovation. As I said, all it takes is managers and supervisors taking the trouble to show that they care."

"That sounds good," Charlie said. "I'm convinced, but if I take this approach back to my executive team, it's going to be helpful to have some sort of evidence to back me up."

"I think you already have the evidence you need," Tom replied. "I know you have *First, Break All the Rules* on your shelf. We discussed it at lunch. Do you have it handy?" Charlie scanned his bookshelf, pulled the volume, and handed it to Tom.

"One of the first things the Gallup researchers who wrote the book did was to develop a survey," Tom said, as he thumbed through the book. "That's what Gallup does, right? They put together dozens of yes-or-no questions that they posed to employees at multiple companies. At the same time, they rated the companies on four business outcomes: productivity, profitability, retention, and customer satisfaction. They found that, of all the questions they asked, there were 12—when answered in the affirmative—that correlated with companies that performed highly in at least one of those four outcomes.

"And what were those key questions?" Tom asked rhetorically, opening to a page. "Let me read them to you:

The Third Domain of Organizational Excellence

1. Do I know what is expected of me at work?

2. Do I have the materials and equipment I need to do my work right?

3. At work, do I have the opportunity to do what I do best every day?

4. In the last seven days, have I received recognition or praise for good work?

5. Does my supervisor or someone at work seem to care about me as a person?

6. Is there someone at work who encourages my development?

7. At work, do my opinions seem to count?

8. Does the missions/purpose of my company make me feel like my work is important?

9. Are my coworkers committed to doing quality work?

10. Do I have a best friend at work?

11. In the last six months, have I talked with someone about my progress?

12. At work, have I had opportunities to learn and grow?

"You can see that at least six or seven of the questions are directly linked to managers making their employees feel valued, cared about, or paid attention to. You get the idea."

"Okay, I'm with you," said Charlie. "Let's sum up. What do we have so far?"

"If I hear you correctly, people more or less felt safe and supported under Jim," Tom said. "There wasn't a real plan in place. It was just a matter of personal style. Jim made people feel good about working here. And the way responsibilities were divided, he left it to Bob and Henry to hold people accountable. Again, we're not talking about a deliberate strategy; it's just the way things worked out."

Lee picked up the thread. "When Bob took over, things went downhill. You had accountability without support. As a result, your employees now feel less safe and more insecure. In these circumstances, it's hard, almost impossible, for them to do their best to provide high-quality medical care. Showing initiative and taking responsibility for tasks not strictly listed in their job description are too risky, so they just keep their heads down and work. The first thing to go is any attempt to make others feel cared for. The second is top-notch technical performance, in your case, medical care. The MRSA outbreak is the first major symptom of this, but I'll bet you could find similar problems simmering throughout the organization. We could back up your assessment with a staff survey, but I think it's clear what you would find."

"And here's another connection that we haven't made," Tom said. "In the absence of a deliberate, Dominion-wide effort to make staff feel supported, staff identify with the part of the organization that seems most caring—and that's usually their own unit—so you heard people refer to themselves as being part of the surgery team or the cancer team. These are generally good units. But when people don't feel they have any personal support, like that nurse in pediatrics, the one who complained to you about her computer, they are going to feel frustrated, resentful, and abandoned."

"And it's clear you have a more immediate problem as well," Lee pointed out. "The members of your executive team also feel frustrated and resentful. Some, in fact, feel abandoned. Your medical director as good as told you that if things don't change soon, he was going to look somewhere else. That's pretty serious. It also seems that gender and generational issues compound the divisions on the team. That seating pattern that everyone has fallen into is pretty revealing. The old boys have set the agenda and the women have been, until now, unwilling to confront them. This may not be premeditated, but it's there nonetheless."

"I came into this meeting feeling pretty optimistic," said Charlie with a sigh. "Now, I'm feeling pretty depressed. We have our work cut out for us."

"That's true," Lee responded, "but I think people at Dominion want it to be a better place, and at least some of them think that you're the guy to move Dominion in the right direction."

"So what's next?" Charlie asked.

"The next step is to start looking at how the human need for safety and security plays out in groups," Tom said. "In a way, we need to widen our assessment. As children, we looked for safety and security in the family. A healthy family provides the kind of stability and support we need to flourish—and we bring our understanding of family dynamics to groups that we join later in life, whether it's the volunteer fire company or the teams at work. We've seen evidence of the attachment process at Dominion. Now we need to explore how it works."

"That's right. There are two issues to consider during the next stage of our assessment," said Lee. "The first is whether Dominion's staff feels it has a family-like environment. The second is whether teams are functioning well at Dominion. Both of these tie into our third principle."

"I'm ready to give it another try," Charlie replied. "As I've said, I'm not exactly happy with what people have told me, but I've learned a lot in the process."

"And given what you've said about the executive team, maybe it's time for us to sit in on your team meetings," Lee added. "What do you think?"

Tom nodded in agreement, and so did Charlie. "I think that's a good idea," Charlie said. "People already feel they have to watch their backs, and knowing that I have asked two consultants to come into the organization could make them more anxious. Introducing you at our next meeting will be a first step in quieting their fears and moving them along to whatever intervention we decide will work. So I'll look for you on Friday."

The Third Domain of Organizational Excellence

Principle 2: People are most productive in an emotionally safe and supportive environment.

1. In the work environment, people need to feel safe, secure, and attached to others. This is a survival mechanism that has evolved over time and is hard-wired into the brain. People feel this need in all aspects of their lives, at home and at work. Satisfying needs for safety, security, and attachment preempts logical thought.

2. People perceive threats to safety and security as rejection. In an organization, these threats can take various forms, from potential layoffs to critical performance reviews. In addition, these threats can be real or perceived. People can even interpret indifference or inattention as a threat. Regardless, such threats may have such a powerful effect on people that financial rewards do not compensate for them. When people feel that they are not cared for, they may become angry, defensive, and withdrawn, and the quality of their work suffers. Or they may choose to leave.

3. Managers can meet their employees' need for safety and security in the workplace by showing that they care for them and their work. Knowing that a supervisor accepts them, supports their efforts, listens to them, encourages their development, and pays attention to their performance strengthens employees' feelings of attachment to the organization. Only in a caring and supportive culture do people show initiative, challenge accepted wisdom, and take intellectual and creative risks. Accordingly, a caring and supportive culture correlates closely with an organization's success.

CHAPTER 3

PEOPLE WORKING TOGETHER TEND TO REPLICATE FAMILY STRUCTURES AND DYNAMICS

Charlie sat at his desk staring out at the parking lot and watching the shadow of the hospital's new wing—Jim's wing—stretch out across the pavement as the afternoon drew to a close. He was thinking about what Tom and Lee had just told him about families and the innate drive for security. It had been a long time since he had practiced family medicine, but he had seen enough to know that there were families where children received the support and encouragement they needed to grow into secure, confident young adults, where their need for attachment was satisfied. That was a real pleasure to see. And then there were families where, for one reason or another, something was missing, and the children struggled to find themselves. He wondered what sort of families he would encounter during his examination of the departments at Dominion.

Before Lee and Tom left, they suggested a few questions he could ask people: Do you think of yourself as part of a team? Do you think most people you work with care about you as a person? Do people seem to appreciate your ideas and your work? Do you trust the people you work with? Do they treat you fairly? He would try them out and see what he learned.

Charlie understood that Lee and Tom were not suggesting that Dominion needed to be one big, happy family. Not at all. Rather, they proposed that managers acknowledge a key element of the people side of business. If people came to Dominion—or any organization they joined—hard-wired to look for the kinds of security and support potentially found in families, it was the responsibility of the CEO to respond to this impulse and use it to the organization's advantage.

A good place to start, Charlie decided, would be orthopedics. The turnover rate in that department was higher than in any other department at the hospital—and it might be a good idea to find out why. He had his assistant make an appointment for him to visit the head of orthopedics, Andy Benjamin, as well as several other department heads.

Investigating Family Dynamics in Orthopedics

The next morning at 10 sharp, Charlie entered Andy Benjamin's office. Andy's expensively decorated office was always scrupulously neat. Charlie didn't know that much about art, but he was sure the framed print over the red lacquer console table was a Matisse—and it didn't look like a reproduction. Andy was reputed to have some money of his own, but it was equally true that he was a very successful orthopedic surgeon. Andy asked him if he wanted some coffee, pointing to the china coffee set on the console, but Charlie turned him down. "Already had my quota of caffeine for the morning," he said.

Andy placed great stock in these little formalities, and Charlie supposed there was no particular harm to them, but they never seemed to be particularly genuine. It was just that for Andy, as a person and as a physician, the forms were important. There was a right way to do things and a wrong way. Andy liked doing things the right way, which in most cases was his way.

"Andy," Charlie began, "no one knows this department better than you. You've transformed it into one of the best in the region in the 10 years since Jim recruited you. But I've noticed that the turnover rate among your nursing staff is higher than anywhere else in the hospital, and it has been high for a long time. What do you think is going on?"

"I don't really know," said Andy. "I used to worry about it, but now I just accept it as a fact of life. There doesn't seem much I can do about it anyway, and it doesn't seem to hurt our performance."

Charlie kept his focus, determined not to be sidetracked. "Do people in your department get along well?" Charlie asked. "Do you think orthopedics functions as real team?"

Andy took a second to respond. "Do you mean my surgical teams? In my opinion, they are second to none. Our nurses have a great deal of respect for our physicians, I can assure you. They are adept at following the lead of the doctors, and so far we have turned in superior results. It is a wonderful system. I am very proud of the teamwork they display."

It dawned on Charlie that his definition of teamwork and Andy's were totally different. Andy saw teams as groups of people who came together to carry out a task. Charlie saw them as communities. "Okay, but do you think the nurses are proud to be part of the team?" Charlie asked.

That question stopped Andy in his tracks. "You know, I've never really thought of that," he said. "My goal is to maintain an efficient, well-run department. I suppose they feel proud. I have honestly never asked them." A tone of uncertainty had crept into Andy's voice. Charlie thought he saw a real person behind the fussy exterior, a physician who was concerned about helping people and doing a good job. He also sensed in Andy a willingness to at least consider something new—and that was a good sign.

"I'm interested in the broader view, Andy, how your whole department functions together. It's at least a possibility that your high rate of turnover is related to your staff not feeling as if they are part of the group, not feeling as if the role they play in your success is ever recognized. That might be why people leave. Tell me, when was the last time you brought the whole orthopedics team together to recognize your nurses and technicians for their accomplishments?"

"I really can't remember," said Andy, sounding a bit deflated. "I assumed that helping physicians care for patients was its own reward."

Charlie had heard the same comment from Lou Perrott. "Let me ask you another question," he said. "Do you think your patients are satisfied with the care they get?"

"Well, they should be," Andy replied defensively. "Our results are among the best in the state."

"But do they feel cared for as people?" Charlie asked.

"That's hard to say. With the current system of reimbursement, we have to push people through the hospital as quickly as possible. We do more outpatient surgery than ever before, and, more often than not, patients are in pain when they leave. They probably feel like we push them out before they're ready, but there's not too much we can do about that. There simply isn't much of an opportunity for my physicians or nurses to build much of a relationship with their patients."

Andy paused for a second. "You know, Charlie, I can see where you are going with this, and intellectually it makes sense to me. I'm not sure, given the system, how to change the culture in the department."

"To be absolutely honest, Andy, I'm not sure either. It might have something to do with creating the kind of supportive, caring atmosphere you find in good families, but I don't quite yet see how to translate that insight into practice. I'll keep you posted, though. You run a superb department, and I'm just trying to find ways to make it even better, and in turn make the hospital better."

As he ushered Charlie out of the office, Andy shook his hand with some feeling. Charlie was surprised. Maybe Andy had been looking for someone who cared enough about his work to ask him some tough questions about it.

Walking back to his office, Charlie thought about what Tom and Lee had said at their first meeting about the three dimensions of a successful business. Like so many companies, Dominion had focused on technical and financial excellence. Given that emphasis, there was no real incentive for department heads to create a family atmosphere, where both staff and patients felt cared for. It was up to him to turn that around.

An Employee Grievance

Sally Heally, Dominion's vice president for human resources, started to get up when Charlie walked through the door of his outer office on his way back from talking to Andy. "Can you give me five minutes?" he asked, heading into his office.

"Sure, sure," she said, looking a bit confused. Sally had scheduled an appointment with Charlie to discuss a recent grievance by a member of the oncology staff. Charlie knew that, but he wanted to jot down his thoughts about the meeting with Andy while they were still fresh. A few minutes later, he reappeared and welcomed her into his office.

"I'm sorry," he said, as they sat down. "I sometimes get so caught up in my plans for the hospital that I forget my manners."

"Oh, I understand," said Sally. "But I appreciate your mentioning it."

Sally gathered her thoughts. "This is complicated," she said. "Joyce Williams, a longtime nurse in oncology, has filed a formal grievance with my department for having been denied promotion to unit manager. She claims age discrimination."

"In oncology?" said Charlie in surprise. "You mean Ryan Albert's unit?"

"That's right," said Sally. "Here's the story. A nurse with less seniority—better qualified in every way—got the promotion that Joyce, the nurse filing the grievance, assumed should be hers. In addition to her technical skills, the newer nurse is a natural leader and gets along well with just about everyone on the floor. In contrast, Joyce is viewed as distant, rigid, and demanding."

"What about the selection process?" Charlie asked. "Was it fair?"

"Ryan did it by the book," Sally said. "A selection committee that consisted of department members and senior staff from other departments at the hospital chose Kerry Stanton—and Joyce had every opportunity to present her case. Ryan agreed with their choice."

"And Joyce. What's the story with her?"

"Well," Sally replied, "this is what I mean about it being complicated. This hospital is her whole life. She has worked here for 25 years. Her children are grown, and her husband runs a very successful venture capital fund and is often out of town. He has donated a significant amount of money to the hospital; I would expect he did so because she wanted him to. Making it more complicated is that both Joyce and her husband socialized with Jim at fundraising events over the years, so I wouldn't be surprised if she thought that the unit manager position would naturally be hers when it came open."

Charlie was frowning now. "Does she have any chance of succeeding with the complaint?"

"I don't think so," said Sally. "I've spent a fair amount of time since I came on board tightening our procedures for hiring and promotion. And fairness is really important to Ryan. As I said, he did it by the book."

"How's he been handling this?"

"My impression from working with Ryan on the MRSA plan is that he feels that the hospital has not supported him the way it should. He is very dedicated. He's built a first-rate department with a reputation for being the best place in the region to get cancer care, not simply because of the expert team he's assembled but because he has made it a warm and inviting place, both for his staff and for his patients. That's very important to him—and I think he considers the budget cutbacks a sign that the hospital doesn't share his vision for the department."

Charlie nodded. He had heard Ryan say essentially the same thing, though he wasn't going to tell Sally that. "What's your point?"

"When I talked to him about it, he focused almost entirely on Kerry, on her qualifications for the job, and how he ran a fair, impersonal selection process. I think he assumed that the fairness of the process would speak for itself and that Joyce would just accept the results. I don't think he was particularly sympathetic when he told her that she didn't get the job—and now that Joyce has filed a grievance, he sees it as another attack on his integrity."

"This doesn't strike me as typical," Charlie said. "I'm doing an assessment with Tom and Lee to determine if the departments provide a supportive family-like environment for their staff, and I didn't think to talk to Ryan, because he seems really attuned to the needs of his employees."

"I think you're right. He holds regular team meetings where everyone, I'm told, is welcome to participate and does. The staff has periodic potluck dinners and hosts a great Christmas party. Equally important, he has a clear vision of quality care in the department. Every member of his team has a role to play, and they all seem eager to perform it."

Charlie made up his mind. "So the bottom line is that Ryan might have headed this off by spending more time with Joyce when she was passed over for promotion. I'll talk to him about that and get his sense of what went on. In the meantime, someone needs to reach out to Joyce even while the grievance is in process. She's worked hard for the hospital, she's clearly going through some sort of transition in her life, and she deserves some support. Would you sit down with her and just talk to her about how she's feeling?"

"Sure. I would be happy to meet with her. And I'll let you know how it goes." Sally paused. "By the way, people are noticing that you have been walking around, asking questions."

"Oh, really?" Charlie said. "What are they saying?"

"There is a wide range of reactions. Some are thrilled to see the boss and are gratified that you're interested in what they have to say. Others are worried that you're checking up on them. And some assume that any new leader should be getting to know his staff and their programs."

Charlie thought about this for a second. "Here you have three different interpretations of the same basic action. Personalities clearly drive the way people think about what I've been doing—and I'd be a fool if I didn't recognize that."

Sally didn't know exactly how to respond to that, but she thought Charlie was thinking about the right issues. "He's a good guy to work for," she thought to herself. "It's going to be interesting to see if he can change things at Dominion."

Charlie stood up, a clear signal that the meeting was over, and walked with Sally to the door. "Thanks for keeping me posted about the grievance," he said. "Let me know how your talk with Joyce goes. Make it clear to her that we're not trying to talk her out of pursuing the grievance, just interested in her well-being as a dedicated employee, okay?"

"Sure thing," said Sally, nodding at Henry Powell, Dominion's CFO, as she passed through the office.

The CFO Reports

Charlie looked at Henry and grinned. "Next," he said, moving his arm in a gracious sweep toward his inner office. Charlie had developed a genuine fondness for Henry. Henry was dedicated to Dominion and viewed his financial skills, which were considerable, as a way of protecting and strengthening it. And, Charlie believed, he was a good person to have on his executive team. Although he was conservative by nature—a good quality to have in your CFO—he was, within limits, curious. Charlie had the feeling that Henry gave new ideas a fair hearing.

Henry began the meeting by reviewing the latest financials. The numbers were holding stable despite the MRSA problems, and the hospital was maintaining its market share. "So far, so good," thought Charlie.

However, Henry was concerned not so much about the immediate effect of MRSA, but about what it represented. "We can't be siphoning off our profits to deal with MRSA or to train new nurses," he said. "The reimbursement picture is getting grimmer and grimmer, and our margins are already under pressure. In this business, you have to invest in technology just to keep market share. And if you can't grow, you're not going to generate the revenue to invest in facilities."

The Third Domain of Organizational Excellence

Charlie was nodding his head. "You're absolutely right, Henry, but the issue goes beyond immediate profit and loss. Unless we transform the hospital into a high-performance organization, unless we start acting like a team, we're never going to reduce the drag on our bottom line, and we're never going to be able to grow efficiently. This is the point I've been trying to make at our executive team meetings."

"So we're really talking about a long-term investment in quality and productivity," Henry said. "Let me think about that. In the meantime, you might be interested to know I've just instituted a number of changes that will improve the performance of our billing team."

Charlie was all ears. "That's great," he said. "If we're going to improve customer satisfaction, we have to get the billing department on board. After all, every patient at the hospital and, in many cases, some of their family members, come in contact with the billing department. It has a tremendous influence on how the marketplace perceives Dominion, because there are few things that cause more anxiety than money. We can go to great lengths to provide wonderful care, but if someone has a bad experience with billing, our reputation goes out the window. So, what's going on?"

"Well," Henry began, "one of the things that affects the way people think about their jobs is their work environment. Are their computers up to date? Are their surroundings attractive? When the company invests in their surroundings, people feel valued."

"I couldn't agree more," Charlie said. Henry seemed to be getting it.

"In all honesty, we had neglected the billing department, and those offices were starting to look pretty shabby. I guess we figured, except for the intake areas, no one sees where they work, so what difference does it make?

"But now I can see the limits of that approach. We've found a home for the old desks at an afterschool program, brought in new computers, and installed these beautiful new cubicles and chairs. The staff members have their own comfortable place to work, better privacy, and fewer distractions. We've also developed standardized protocols for them to deal with accounts."

Charlie quickly saw that, while a start, Henry's appreciation of the issues facing the billing department still had a ways to go. "Clearly the changes you made should result in greater efficiency," Charlie said after a few seconds. "That's good. But I'm not sure getting our folks new equipment and putting people in cubicles is the answer to promoting teamwork or that it will in itself move us closer to being a high-performance organization."

He could tell Henry was feeling a little let down. "Seriously, Henry, consider it a good first step. Keep your eyes on it and let's be prepared to do some fine-tuning." He looked at his watch. "It's almost six. I don't know where these days go. I'm heading out. Walk you over to the parking lot?"

"Thanks, Charlie," Henry said. "I have a few things to clear off my desk before I leave. I'll see you at the executive team meeting."

On the way home, Charlie thought more about Henry. He had good intentions, but it was going to take some time and patience to bring folks like Henry over to the people side of business. Charlie had the patience. He just didn't know if he had the time.

Family Matters at Dominion

Charlie had scheduled a meeting with Tom and Lee on Friday morning, an hour before they were all to go into the executive team meeting. He had devoted two hours on Thursday to meeting with a series of department heads and getting a sense of their approach to teamwork. His conversations mostly confirmed his sense that his leaders thought of teams as a mechanism to achieve a specific task: quality medical care. It was not surprising, given these circumstances, that people were not giving their all for Dominion. And when he specifically raised the issue of creating a family-like environment at Dominion, they heard him out politely, but noncommittally.

Consequently, he was glad to see Tom and Lee when they walked into his office. He was getting a better sense of the obstacles Dominion faced and knew he was going to need their insights. "You know, you two are spending enough time at Dominion that I should find an office for you," he said.

Tom laughed. "That would then defeat the whole purpose of hiring consultants," he said. "Much of our value for you comes from our *not* being part of your organization. And having an office down the hall, while convenient, would make things that much harder for us to see Dominion objectively."

"Tom's right, as usual," Lee said. "But tell us what you've been finding out."

Charlie briefed them on his meetings with Andy Benjamin and the other department heads. He also told them about his conversations with Sally and Henry.

"It was fascinating to listen to Andy talk about his surgical teams," Charlie continued. "Like many of the department heads I spoke to, he focuses almost exclusively on outcomes— and as long as they're good, he's happy. At least initially, he was oblivious to the family and team issues I was trying to bring up. It just never occurred to him that his staff might benefit from recognition as people.

"Like Lou, he lets himself off the hook by asserting that doing good works is its own reward. While I agree, it also makes sense to me to reward and support people for their good works, and that if you create teams that harness everyone's potential, you can do exceptional things for people."

"Let me see if I understand you correctly," Lee said. "Andy is focused intensely on technical issues—which, by the way, is as it should be, given the kind of work he does—but he lets it blind him to the emotional responses that people are hard-wired to bring to every situation, including the operating room. He's not supportive because he sees no reason to be so. It's no wonder he's oblivious to the causes of his attrition problems or that the MRSA outbreak seems completely inexplicable to him." Lee smiled and added, "What he can't explicate, he cannot eradicate."

"But I don't want to be too hard on Andy," Charlie replied. "What I found fascinating in my conversation with him was that he, too, has an emotional side. I thought of him as a bit of a stuffed shirt, but by the time I left, I had a sense that behind Andy's formal manner was someone who really wanted to make a difference and who might be willing to consider new perspectives."

"That's a good point," said Lee. "People like Andy tend to hide their emotions, and, as you've found out, you sometimes have to make a special effort to see their emotional side. But it's there. There's no exception to this particular rule."

"Talking to Andy and the other department heads gave me a lot to think about," Charlie said. "For instance, now that I'm looking at things in terms of teams and supportive family structure, I'm bowled over by the hierarchical way things are set up here. I'm a physician, and of course I know that docs like to run things, but it was eye opening to take a fresh look at how things work. It's not so much that Andy's surgeons are in charge, but it's their attitude that struck me. Certainly, each person has and should have a well-defined role in a surgical procedure, but the docs view the nurses not as part of the team but as their servants. It's like a family that tells the children, "Speak but only when spoken to." That kind of situation is not exactly conducive to good teamwork and optimal performance."

"I noticed that you found it easy to compare surgical teams to families," said Tom jumping in. "That's exactly our point. Family dynamics are important at work, not because the work environment is intrinsically like a family, but because people come to work—really to any group—expecting it to operate like one. It's the frame of reference that we've been hard-wired by evolution to have. We've evolved to find safety and security through families, and we see the world that way. You can't stop people from looking at everything through the lens of family any more than you can stop people from having emotions. It's simply a fact of life, and if you're a manager, you ignore this fact at your own peril.

"Which gets me," Tom continued, "back to our third principle: *People working together tend to replicate family structures and dynamics.* People naturally want to feel connected to their organization and its mission, just as they want to feel connected to their family. They bring the same techniques and the same emotional tools to achieve this aim at work as they do in a family.

"This principle is simply an extension of the science that underlies the essential human need for nurturance. People attach to one or two caregivers, usually their parents, for survival. Successful attachment is critical to their development as people, which is why children fare better in foster homes than they do in orphanages. In the work environment, people apply this fundamental tendency for attachment to one or two supervisors. Humans impose this model on group relationships.

"The business research from *First, Break All the Rules* confirms these concepts. Employees want a supervisor to care about them, praise them, and encourage their development. Successful managers understand that creating an environment that provides some of the support people find in families is critical for having people feel involved and committed. It also frees people to give their best to the organization."

"I think I understand what you're talking about from my practice of family medicine," said Charlie. "But what kinds of things do people look for when they apply their family perspective at work?"

"For starters, people want a value system that strikes a chord with them," Tom said. "When an organization's goals are aligned with their personal values, they feel comfortable and safe. They will contribute when they feel in concert with these goals and resist when they're not.

"There are other things that people are looking for," Tom continued, "but before we go too far, I really need to stress my point that organizations are *not* families. There are some very important distinctions. People are born into a family, but they earn their place in an organization. You don't get dismissed from a family, but you can be fired from your job for poor performance. Both families and business environments should provide acceptance, support, opportunities for development, and structure. But the organization demands—rightly—performance for continued membership."

"I thought that was where you were headed," Charlie said. "So you are not saying we should turn Dominion into a family?"

"Absolutely not," Tom replied. "Rather, our point is that because people are hard-wired to see the organizations they're part of as a family, organizations should respond by providing some of the emotional support that people look for in a family."

"Let's get back on track," Lee said. "Tom mentioned that people look to organizations for the kind of shared value system they gain from families. Another thing that people look for in organizations that comes from the family is fair process. Kids constantly scrutinize their parents' decisions to see if they're fair. When people don't feel they are being treated fairly, they become angry and resentful. The same thing is true on the job. When the work environment is fair, people feel relaxed and secure. They can even tolerate being passed over for promotion if they feel the process was fair."

"I understand that, but what happened with Joyce Williams and Ryan Albert? Ryan created a very supportive family atmosphere in oncology, ran a fair and transparent promotion process, and yet Joyce filed a grievance."

"That's right," Lee responded, "but we're back again to personality. Every employee has a unique approach to attachment, both at home and at work, that was determined by their genes and by the degree to which they felt cared for and attached in their own family. Joyce's husband is away a lot and her children have left home. Although it was not the only response open to her, Joyce invested herself, and her family money, in the oncology department. She effectively treated the department as if it were her family and viewed the promotion as an affirmation of her value. Not every person would act this way. Unfortunately for her, the department is part of a business—It's not a family—and she has to earn her promotion.

"At the same time," Lee went on, "Ryan has the responsibility as an effective leader to treat Joyce with compassion, enabling her to adjust to her failure. Like Lou and Andy, he took refuge in an abstraction—in this case an intellectual notion of fairness that he as an African American might have especially valued—and used it as a substitute for emotional support. Joyce may not have had the skills to earn the promotion, but nonetheless she has been a valuable contributor to the department. Ryan's role is to create a supportive environment. It was his job to remind Joyce that she is valued for her good work, making it possible for her to accept the decision. How she ultimately acts is up to her."

"Let me see if I can connect the dots," said Charlie. "Ryan feels under attack from Bob and Henry, who he feels are withdrawing their support. He reacts defensively by withdrawing his support from his staff, at least in this case. And now Joyce feels under attack by him. It's a vicious cycle."

"And Ryan can break that cycle," Lee responded. "He can do that by acknowledging Joyce's disappointment and making a reasonable attempt to help her adjust. He can do this himself, get support from Sally's group in HR, or call on outside consultants."

"But to give Ryan his due," Tom added, "it's sometimes very difficult for leaders to anticipate the particular emotional reactions of their staff. It's equally difficult to respond after the fact, especially in a situation like Ryan's, where he felt his integrity was questioned."

"You know, Charlie," Lee continued, "it falls to you to help Ryan come to terms with his personal reaction to Joyce's grievance. And it's also a way for you to demonstrate to the members of your executive team that emotions must be acknowledged at Dominion."

Viewing Work through the Lens of Family

Tom considered Charlie thoughtfully for a second. "There are a number of other well-known implications for managers when people view the work environment through the lens of family. Your personal example is important, not simply because you are the CEO but because people automatically view supervisors like you as parent substitutes. How this plays out in individual cases depends on a person's experience. In most cases, it will mean that they will look for guidance and support, but if they have had a bad experience with their parents, they may transfer that resentment to their supervisor."

"So whatever they experienced gets pasted on me?" It made Charlie a little uncomfortable.

"That's about it," Tom said. "It's a daunting realization—and there's nothing you can do about it, at least initially—but if you're consistent and fair and supportive, workers may, over time, come to see you for who you are and not as a parent.

"The tendency to see the workplace through the lens of family has other implications," Tom added. "Not only do employees see their supervisors as parents but they also see peers as siblings, which accounts for a lot of the petty rivalry that you see at work. And they see subordinates as children. This is normal human behavior and something managers should expect.

"And here's another way that people's experience of family affects the workplace. The research on attachment tells us that people are more comfortable working in small groups because of their resemblance to their original families. This occurs in the largest of organizations. For example, in the military, operations are usually organized by forces the size of a battalion or larger, but the functional unit is the squad, which is made up of 9 to 10 people."

The Third Domain of Organizational Excellence

Charlie looked puzzled. "You're telling me that we should work in small teams, but haven't we been saying that the problems at Dominion, like the MRSA outbreak, are caused in part by the different teams in the hospital operating independently?"

"That's right," Tom replied. "But the problem is not the existence of teams, but teams going off on their own without regard to the larger organization. It's critical for someone in your position to get your executives to function as a team and share the same goals and objectives, something that's not the case now. Right now, your executives are operating as the leaders of their own departmental teams. Once you've built an executive team, your executives can each align their own teams with Dominion's goals."

"That makes sense to me," said Charlie. "If I can get my executive team, for instance, to work together to combat MRSA at Dominion, they will be more effective in bringing their teams to this common effort."

"That's the gist of it," said Tom.

Charlie glanced down at his watch. "Time to get going to the executive meeting," he said. "How about if I introduce the two of you to the team, and you listen in? I've put the people issues we have been talking about at the top of the agenda. And after we're done, we can talk about our next step."

The Executive Team Discusses Quality Healthcare

Charlie felt energized as he walked into the executive meeting. He was beginning to feel ready to tackle people issues at the hospital, and he felt he was developing a framework that would help him. There was more he had to learn—and there were hard decisions ahead about translating Lee and Tom's principles into an action plan—but he was ready and willing. Right now, he felt he had momentum on his side, so as Barry, the last person to arrive, sat down, Charlie jumped right in.

"As you are aware, I have been asking questions around the hospital about the way we treat people at Dominion, both our staff and our patients. From a technical standpoint, Dominion delivers superior care. From a financial perspective, we're in solid shape. But I think we're undermining our technical and financial advantages by neglecting the people side of business. If we don't check the MRSA outbreak and turn it around, if we can't lower our turnover rates, if we continue alienating our patients, then we're jeopardizing our ability to grow, and this institution is doomed to mediocrity. So I've brought in Lee Hersch and Tom DeMaio—organizational consultants as well as psychologists—to help me understand what the people side of business is all about. I'm convinced that change has to start here with the executive team. By working together as a team, we set the agenda for the whole institution."

As often happened before, Bob responded quickly and without hesitation. "We are already a great team. We've made Dominion the successful enterprise it is, and I'm proud of what we accomplished. It was rough when we lost Jim, yet we maintained our dominant position in the market."

"And we have you to thank, Bob, for our doing as well as we have," Charlie said, "but although this team has great people, it's not a real team. We don't really share responsibility for the hospital's struggles. We aren't always open to different points of view. We don't ask for help from one another, or provide constructive feedback. We are group, but I'm not sure we are a team."

The group's response to Charlie's remarks was silence, which surprised him. As he looked around, he thought about how every member of the team had no trouble speaking up when meeting one on one, but when they came together as a group, they lapsed into silence whenever there was some sort of conflict. Then it struck him one more time: He was right; they did not feel secure and they did not function as a team. It was his responsibility to bring them together.

Charlie sensed that he had reached a critical moment and leaned forward in his chair. "As I listened to our discussions over the four months since I came on board, I've noticed that each of you assumes, however tacitly, that if your department is free to do what you think best, then we'll end up with quality medical care. I couldn't disagree more.

"I respect your diverse opinions—In fact, I need you to bring your different viewpoints to our discussions—but I also need your commitment to a collective vision for the hospital. What does that mean? It means that you need to think about your areas in terms of what is good for the hospital. When you do so, you will see the opportunity to address the broader issues such as positive patient experiences, seamless transitions from one service to another, and consistency across departments that we need to address if we're to take Dominion to the next level.

"We're the executive team. It's up to us to create the kind of mutually supportive atmosphere on this team that you find in the best families. And we have to think about creating this type of atmosphere for our staff and our customers. In the final analysis, this leadership team must change if this hospital is to succeed."

There was another pause. As he had in previous meetings, Henry filled the gap. "I'm very worried this will hurt our bottom line," he said.

Charlie looked directly at Henry. He understood that Henry was interested in change, but also afraid of it. "You know, Henry, that if we don't do something soon, our bottom line is going to suffer, and we're not going to have much of a future. If the leadership team can come together around the mission of the hospital and the people side of business, then I promise you the bottom line will be well served."

There was another pause, and then Sally spoke up. "I, for one, would be thrilled to see this happen. One of the things I saw when Ryan and I worked together was how much we accomplished—and how many new ideas we generated. Tackling MRSA is serious business, but I have to admit I found it extremely satisfying collaborating on the plan."

Julie looked across the table at Bob and Henry to give force to what she was going to say. "I also agree with Charlie. From a marketing point of view, working together as a team would make my job—all our jobs—that much easier."

Charlie could tell from the expression on his face that Bob was clearly monitoring the direction of the discussion—and it was clear that he didn't like where it was going. "With all due respect, Charlie, this approach concerns me. Jim wanted everyone to be happy, which made it difficult to hold people accountable, but I managed to do that for him. Now you want us to make it a priority to make people happy just at the moment when we have to contend with the MRSA outbreak. I think we need to take care of business."

Charlie was about to reply when Ryan jumped in. He too had been listening closely to the conversation. "Bob, I know this hospital means a lot to you, but your sense of our options is too limited," he began. "That's something I've learned in treating people with cancer. You can't just focus on the medical and technical aspects of delivering care. The nature of cancer treatment requires that we address people's attitudes and motivation, not just their tumors. Even in the best of circumstances, a person with cancer has a difficult road to follow. They have to deal with surgery, chemo, even radiation—and if we want them to get the most out of their treatment, we need to provide them the emotional support they need to persevere. We've talked about this before, but it's still true. You get better results, whether you're running an oncology department or a hospital, when you pay attention to people's emotions and plan accordingly."

Charlie decided it was time to end the discussion for today. "We are not going to resolve this issue right now, but I would like you to give some thought to what I've been saying. I know each of you feels passionately committed to what you believe is best for Dominion. I want you to know as we continue these discussions that I very much respect and appreciate that commitment."

Charlie looked at the faces around the table and then down at his watch. "Okay, we have a number of reports to hear before we adjourn. Henry, do you want to update us on the financials?"

As Henry stood up to make his presentation, Ryan caught Charlie's eye and nodded almost imperceptibly. Ryan had made his decision.

The Power of Teams

Lee and Tom lingered as the members of the executive team gathered up their papers. As Barry was about to slip through the door, Charlie stopped him. "Barry, did you have a chance to send someone over to talk to that nurse in pediatrics about her computer issues?" he asked.

Barry looked faintly annoyed. "I have it on my to-do list," he said, "but I don't want to divert manpower from the electronic medical record project."

"*Man*power! Don't you have any women on your staff?" Charlie asked, half jokingly, but when Barry looked blank, he simply said, "See that you get to it this week, okay?" Barry nodded and left the room.

Charlie shrugged and turned to Tom and Lee. "How did you think the meeting went?" he asked.

"Well, you have your team engaged," said Tom. "Whether they agree or not, they're listening to you. And there are clearly a number of members who want you to move in the new direction. Sure, you heard from the predictable naysayers, but the other team members took them on. What did *you* think?"

"I think it's a real start. I have the feeling some of the team is willing to step up and take some responsibility for our new direction. It won't all be on my shoulders."

Lee nodded. "I think you're right. A few of the key players are not convinced, and there is the predictable resistance, but the fact that you're beginning to have an open debate, where everyone is focused on the greater good of Dominion as a whole, is a sign that they are moving in the right direction. And a good team, especially at the leadership level, can give an organization the advantage it needs to outperform competitors with more resources."

"Collins makes exactly that point in *Good to Great*," said Charlie, thoughtfully. "He says that making a good company great requires a dynamic team at the top. The leader wants great people around him and expects the team to determine the direction of the company. He says that good to great management teams thrive on vigorous debate, yet unify behind decisions, regardless of the interests of the individual executives."

"And here's why teams are so powerful," Tom said. "Teams are the closest you can come in an organization to replicating the sense of security and togetherness you find in a family. Teams are the answer to what people are looking for when they come to work. Good teams—teams in which people are treated fairly and with respect—replicate the safety that we found tens of thousands of years ago living in small groups of trusted family members and friends. Managers who recognize this principle have a powerful tool at their disposal that can maximize the potential of their organizations. Because it's hard-wired, it's easy to overlook it, but it's incredibly potent.

"Before the meeting, we were talking about the idea that people look to organizations for the common value system and the sense of fair play they found in families. They also want to trust the organization—their teammates in particular—just the way they trust their family. That feeling of trust is a signal that you are safe and connected to the group and there is no threat of rejection. You're home. When there's no trust, teams become dysfunctional, just like families that lack trust. To have trust, you have to have acceptance, mutual support and commitment, and fair process. When people feel trusted and trust the organization, you have a powerful instrument for growth. Your goal as a manager is to create the framework in which trust can flourish."

"A very important advantage of creating an environment where trust can flourish," added Lee, "is that individual and team goals start aligning with organizational goals. This too is a function of evolution. Given the opportunity, we build families of families—clans and tribes—that share the same values. But people have to feel trust for this to happen."

Charlie took a second to process all this. "How does this trust get established?" he asked.

"Let me take a stab at answering that," Tom said. "Before the meeting, Lee mentioned that people see their supervisors as parent figures. Right now, that's you—and what you do is critical in establishing trust. In fact, part of the problem with Dominion is that Bob was not very good at being a parent.

"When Bob came on board, he wanted everyone to toe the line—his line. If you look at what happened from a family perspective, you can see what went wrong. Essentially, Bob's threat to withhold approval if he found performance lacking, coupled with Jim's sudden disappearance, made Dominion seem like a dangerous place. The women on your team, Sally, Debbie, and Julie, sensed that Bob was failing to provide safety and security. They were afraid to confront him, because they considered him a distant, critical parent. They retreated into silence."

"That seems so obvious now that you point it out," Charlie said. "Clearly I need to give some thought to the kind of parent I want to be. It's not something I learned at business school, but since people reflexively see me as a parent figure, I guess I should be a good one. I didn't realize how powerfully my leadership style would affect my staff."

"And you're not the only leader at Dominion," Tom continued. "There are scores of teams at the hospital—in places like billing and marketing, in the operating rooms, and on the units. In each case, you're going to need leaders who work hard to establish trust, encourage free and open disagreement, provide individual support, and emphasize accountability and attention to results."

"We've talked about Bob as a parent," Charlie interjected, "but what about Jim? I had the feeling that he established trust, but I don't know. I'm not sure I want to be a parent figure like Jim, either."

"You're right," responded Tom. "Everyone loved and trusted Jim, but Jim fell short in a way that's quite different from Bob: Jim never encouraged the people on his team to act independently and to play a role in leading the organization. In family terms, no one ever asked them to grow up. Jim's staff just assumed he would always be there to set priorities. When Jim left suddenly, everyone—including Bob—was at a loss.

"In a way, our fourth principle—*People want to grow and achieve mastery*—focuses on this failure, but from a slightly different perspective. Jim was a father figure. He was fair and trustworthy, but he didn't help people grow and learn how to take responsibility. One consequence of this was that there was no one qualified to step into his shoes when he became sick."

Tom looked at his watch. "You've given a good deal of your time to this project today, and you're setting the groundwork for some significant change. Why don't you pursue your investigations next week about how Dominion supports the growth and development of its staff? We're not just interested in workshops and training sessions. We're really asking how Dominion helps its staff become mature professionals."

Charlie stood up. "I think I can do that. The point, again, is to think about the staff as individuals, as real people, not tools that I'm trying to refine so that they perform a specific task better."

"Exactly," Lee said. "People have the capacity to take on an enormous range of challenges. In fact, most people embrace the opportunity if they have the chance. It's your job to prepare them to take that chance."

The Third Domain of Organizational Excellence

Principle 3: People working together tend to replicate family structures and dynamics.

1. People are hard-wired to view their work environment much the way they view a family. They naturally want to feel connected to their organization and its mission, just as they want to feel connected to a family. When an organization creates an environment that provides the support people find in healthy families, people feel engaged and committed.

2. People project their unique family experience onto their organization and their leaders. They tend to view supervisors as parent substitutes, peers as siblings, and subordinates as children. The experience they expect depends on the experience they had in their own family of origin. They expect family-like qualities, such as support and structure, from their organization and leaders.

3. Good teams replicate the safety and togetherness found in healthy family experience. People work more naturally in team structures than in hierarchical systems. Teams work best when there is mutual trust, common values, and clear goals.

CHAPTER 4

PEOPLE WANT TO GROW AND ACHIEVE MASTERY

It was still dark as Charlie struggled out in the parking lot, getting the vintage American Airlines poster out of the back seat of his car. He had gone downtown to meet a friend for lunch on Saturday, and because he was early, had decided to browse though a few stores on the downtown mall. He had always loved that angular 1960s style, and when he saw the poster hanging in the corner of a frame shop, he thought, "Well, why not?" It wasn't a Matisse, and it certainly wasn't a harpoon, but he appreciated that Andy and Lou had made their offices their own. It was time he did the same thing. He'd hang it above his conference table. And who knows, he might pick up another one of the vintage airlines posters the store stocked and start a little collection.

As he carried the poster into the building, Charlie thought more about how he would go about pursuing his topic for the week, determining whether Dominion supported the growth and development of its employees. It made sense to get Sally's and Debbie's perspectives. Staff development was Sally's responsibility, and training was particularly important for Debbie's nursing staff. After Tom and Lee had left on Friday, he had had his assistant arrange meetings with Sally and Debbie, and when he checked his schedule over the weekend, he noted that they were set for Wednesday afternoon.

In the meantime, though, Charlie very much wanted to go beyond the executive team and talk to employees themselves. He thought he would drop over to the billing department this morning before the staff settled down to work and talk to a few people there. At the very least, he was curious to see what Henry's new cubicles looked like—and interested to hear what the staff had to say about their new working environment.

Charlie unlocked his office, propped the poster against the wall, turned on his computer, and started working through his e-mail. Half an hour later, he checked his watch: 7:30. Time to get rolling.

Charlie Gets a Perspective on Cubicle Life

The billing department occupied a large, bright, newly painted room, with a series of large windows along the far wall. Across from the entrance were six cubicles, where intake specialists met with patients and family members. Behind them were additional cubicles in pods of four, where the rest of the staff worked. From what he could tell, Henry had more than made up for years of neglect. The cubicles were modern and equipped with a variety of bookcases, cabinets, and desk areas that staff could arrange for their own needs. They looked pretty comfortable.

Charlie introduced himself to the supervisor and told her that he was interested in getting to know a few members of the staff. She referred him to Dan Welch. "I'm pretty new here," the supervisor confessed. "You might do better talking to Dan, who is one of our most experienced people. He's been here quite a while. After you're done, I'm sure he can suggest a few other people you might speak to. He's in the cube at the end of the center aisle near the window."

Charlie walked over to Dan's cubicle and knocked on the wall. A trim man in his late thirties with a bushy mustache looked up at him, surprised. "You're Charlie Fisher, aren't you?

"That I am," said Charlie. "May I sit down?"

"Sure," Dan replied, rising to his feet and pointing to his spare chair. "Make yourself at home. Are you the person we have to thank for our palatial new digs?"

"No, it's not me. It's Henry Powell. He was telling me about them, so I thought I would come and take a look," Charlie replied. "They seem pretty nice. I was wondering what you thought of them?"

"Well," said Dan, after the briefest of pauses. "They're a vast improvement over what we had. They're really quite comfortable. And there's a lot of privacy."

"I can see that," Charlie said looking around, although the small space seemed to be full of people. Wherever there had been some empty wall space, Dan had hung a photograph of a family gathering. Looking around the cubicle, Charlie thought he spotted at least one family reunion, a few weddings, and a 50th anniversary party. "What's the story behind the photographs?" Charlie asked.

Dan paused again before answering. "I don't want to sound ungrateful, because I really appreciate the investment you've made in the cubicles—They're really very nice—but I just started feeling a little lonely sitting here all day, so I thought it would be fun to fill up my cube with pictures of people I care about."

"You have a great-looking family," Charlie said, pointing at a picture of Dan and a young woman his age with three little kids. "But doesn't the department get together as a team?"

"Not really," Dan replied, looking from the photo back to Charlie. "If there's a change in procedure, I'll get an e-mail. We have a staff meeting once a month to go over the big issues, but that's about it. The fact of the matter is, I spent more time with the other people on the team before they put us in these new cubicles."

"How long have you been working in billing?" Charlie asked.

"Six years now."

"And can you put in another six years?"

Dan was taken aback. "I've never thought of that. You know, I hope not," Dan said, though he immediately looked as though he wanted to take his last remark back. "What I mean is, it's not the most fulfilling work in the world."

"It's billing, after all. I'm sure there's an awful lot of repetition," Charlie said. "Do you think you could make it more interesting?"

"I definitely do," Dan replied. "For example, I talk to patients on the phone quite a bit—and I've kept track of the parts of our bills that they find especially confusing. I'd like to see if there was a way to make our bills easier to understand. It would make everyone's life easier. You know how it is. When something isn't clear, patients immediately assume that we're deliberately trying to hide something or put one over on them. We waste a lot of time explaining basic charges that should be obvious."

"So what's the hang up?"

"Well, the hang-up is that no one seems the least bit interested in doing anything differently," Dan replied. "I've asked about seeing if I could form a little task force—nothing special, mind you—to see if there's a simpler way to format our bills, but my managers—and I've had four in the six years I've been here— would rather I just stick to answering the phone. Honestly, I don't think they're interested in what we have to say. That's a shame because there's no one at Dominion who knows more about billing than the billing staff. So the truth of the matter is that I don't really look forward to another six years at Dominion. I feel stuck enough as it is—and although the new cubicles are nice, they don't change any of that."

"So I take it that you don't feel particularly attached to Dominion," Charlie asked.

"Well, I try to do the best job I can," Dan replied, "but I don't think I do it because I feel any particular allegiance to Dominion. I'm sorry, but that's the way it is."

"Don't feel sorry," Charlie said. "I appreciate your speaking frankly. Frank-talking is exactly what I need to get Dominion on course. We're in a competitive business, and we really can't afford to let good ideas go to waste. I'd like to make Dominion a place where anyone who wants to contribute gets a hearing.

"But I think I've taken enough of your time," Charlie stood up. "If you could recommend another person to talk with, I'd appreciate it."

Charlie left the billing department 45 minutes later with a thoughtful look on his face. Everyone he spoke to, like Dan, appreciated the new cubicles, but the consensus was that the cubicles made them feel even more isolated and unsupported. One woman told him that it was very tough to spend 15 minutes on the phone explaining a bill to an irate customer, but the worst part, she had said, was that when the call was over, there was no one to talk to about your experience.

"You feel drained," she had said, "but you're expected to forget about it and move on to the next task." The phrase she used stuck in Charlie's mind: "They expect us to act like robots, not people."

It was a bit of a miracle, Charlie thought, that the billing department functioned as well as it did.

Sally Makes the Case for Human Resources

When Sally arrived for her meeting with Charlie, his assistant was standing across from his desk admiring an arrangement of antique roses he had placed on his desk. "What do you think?" he said, turning to Sally.

Sally looked at it appraisingly. "I like them," she said. "And they smell wonderful. Where did you get them?"

"From my backyard," he said. "I've been growing antique roses for quite some time and have a little greenhouse out there to extend the growing season."

"They certainly are lovely," Sally said. "But why didn't you have them out here earlier in the season?"

"Well, I didn't think it would be okay until a few days ago," he replied. "When it comes to décor, Bob was always on the Spartan side. I didn't think he would have approved, but Charlie is different. Charlie came in on Monday with a vintage American Airlines poster for his office and asked me to help him hang it. While we were at it, we started talking about our hobbies, and I told him about my roses. He encouraged me to bring some in if I wanted to—and I jumped at the chance."

The Third Domain of Organizational Excellence

"I didn't know Charlie collected old posters," Sally remarked.

"Neither did I," said Charlie's assistant. "I guess he does now, though."

As he showed Sally into Charlie's office, she noticed the American Airlines poster above his conference table. "That's really quite nice," she thought. She was beginning to get a sense of Charlie as a real person, not just her boss. "Great poster," she said to Charlie.

Charlie looked pleased. "I thought the office needed a little refreshing," he said.

"I really like it," Sally said. "It gives the office some personality."

Sally paused and went on, "You wanted a little follow-up on the presentation I gave you a few months ago about training opportunities that my department coordinates at Dominion?"

"That's right," said Charlie. "If I remember correctly, you told me that nurses were the primary users of the continuing education and training programs we provide in-house, although they can and do take advantage of opportunities for training at conferences. You said the same was more or less true for administrators and other staff. The physicians, on the other hand, went to training sessions out of the area, and their trips were funded from their departmental budgets."

"That's correct," Sally said. "The expectation is that at Dominion all staff members are to be involved in ongoing training. You know *First, Break All the Rules?*"

"The Gallup book? I was just talking about it with Lee Hersch and Tom DeMaio a few days ago. They're fans."

"I am too," said Sally. "One of the questions that correlates with high-performing organizations is something like 'Do people at work encourage my development, giving me the opportunity to learn and grow?' That's the environment I'm trying to create at Dominion."

"How do you think you've done?" asked Charlie.

"I would give myself a C," she replied. "Jim supported my efforts—We started a number of programs, especially right after I joined the organization—but his priority was on programs that raised the level of technical expertise in the hospital."

"So there hasn't been a lot of focus on what we've been calling the people side of business?"

"That's a fair assessment." Sally answered. "As I said, Jim was always supportive of budgeting training money for skills development, but training for the people side of business wasn't on anyone's radar screen. As the head of HR, I should have pushed harder, but then it became too late. When Bob took over and cut my budget by 30 percent, my focus switched to salvaging as many programs as I could. Despite our efforts, we had to drop a number of them, with nursing taking the bulk of the reductions."

"I wouldn't beat yourself up about this too much," Charlie said. "My impression is that Jim and Bob were not easily swayed once they made up their minds. But how do you think this affected

The Third Domain of Organizational Excellence

Debbie? When we held that first emergency executive team meeting to discuss MRSA, I thought she reacted defensively to Bob's criticism."

"You may want to talk with Debbie directly about that," Sally replied, "but I'm willing to bet she sees the cutbacks as the root cause of all her problems. The nursing training budget was slashed, and she started to lose good people. And because she's lost good people, her staff fails to follow established infection control procedures. That's probably not the whole story, but I would say she feels blamed for a situation that's out of her control."

"That sounds about right," Charlie said, standing up. "I have a meeting with Debbie in an hour to talk about training. I'll follow up with her then. And thanks, Sally, for being so honest about the programs. I have a lot of faith in your ability."

Debbie Expresses Her Frustration

After Sally left, Charlie looked at the pile of paperwork on his desk, sighed, and sat down. Before he knew it, he was deeply engrossed in the work. On the hour, his assistant buzzed and announced that Debbie was there for her appointment. She was exactly on time.

"Have a seat, Debbie," Charlie said showing her into his office, and when she sat down on the very edge of the chair, he added, "make yourself comfortable." Debbie allowed herself to take a deep breath, but didn't relax appreciably.

"I've been meaning to check in to see how you're doing. I know the MRSA outbreak must be upsetting. There has certainly been a lot of pressure on you and your team."

"I appreciate that, Charlie, I really do. We all feel so bad about the outbreak—and so frustrated that it's gone on for so long. I also want to thank you so very much for taking some time to talk with me." Debbie could be nice to a fault.

"No need," said Charlie. "Nursing is critical to the hospital. I had a meeting with Sally today to review training, and I know Bob cut your training budget quite severely in the last year. Do you think this has been an issue in how things are going in your department?"

"It's not just *an* issue," Debbie replied, flaring up suddenly. "It's one of the *biggest* issues." The sudden anger in Debbie's voice took Charlie aback, especially as she had been so accommodating just moments before. "I still can't believe what happened. Bob has no conception of what it's like to keep a nursing staff in this day and age." Charlie saw that he had struck a nerve.

"Nursing is hard, tiring, demanding work—and what keeps most of us going is the chance to improve our skills. Technology is changing all the time, and there's a lot of research now on evidence-based practice. We want to help our patients the best way we can, and training is the way we keep up. When Bob cut the training budget, I think we all took it as an affront; I know I did. Nurses are professionals, after all. And these days, with the nursing shortage, our nurses can easily go elsewhere—and some did, straight to hospitals where they truly value nursing. That made morale even worse, and I think poor morale, more than anything else, is behind the MRSA problem.

"In the old days," Debbie recalled, "Jim always made me feel that I was an important part of the team, even though my office is located far from the administrative wing. He knew how I felt about the importance of training, and he encouraged me to make training a central part of the experience for any nurse here.

"Jim took my professional opinion seriously, but not Bob and Henry. Oh, no." Debbie was getting angry again. "They just pursued their own agendas. To make matters worse, they're totally out of touch with trends in the field today. They think of nursing as woman's work—and if you ask me, they don't have a very high opinion of women. The facts of the matter are that men are entering our profession in increasing numbers and that the level of education among nurses as a group—male and female—is higher today than ever before. It seems to me that by cutting the training budget, Bob and Henry want to return to the good old days—which I can assure you weren't so good."

Now that she had started, Debbie seemed determined to get everything out of her system that had been bothering her. "What it all boils down to," she continued, "is institutional sexism at Dominion, and I don't just mean in the way nurses are treated. It's all over the executive team. For the last year, Bob and Henry effectively excluded the women from the decision-making process. That may not have been their conscious intention, but it's true nonetheless—just ask Julie and Sally—while someone like Barry, who's been delaying the launch of our EMR system for months, simply gets away with murder. It's not fair."

Debbie looked directly at Charlie for a second and then glanced away. She made herself go on. "And when you came, it seemed that you would naturally endorse Bob and Henry's perspective.

I hate to be difficult or contentious, but the women on the executive team have felt completely disenfranchised. You've probably noticed we don't say much in the executive team meetings."

Charlie sat back and thought about how he was going to respond to Debbie. He was moved by the effort it took for her to be direct with him—and he wanted her to know that he appreciated it.

"I'm sorry, Debbie, that you had to go through this," he said. "Let me say first that I'm trying to create an executive team where everyone is an equal contributor. Not only is valuing everyone's contribution and involving the whole team in decision making the right thing to do but it's also what's best for Dominion. If Dominion is to flourish, we are going to need the entire executive team pitching in with their best ideas. We simply can't afford sexism, ageism, racism, or any other "ism" to interfere with this organization taking full advantage of the talent, intelligence, and insight of any member of our staff, regardless of their profession, discipline, or role. As for the budget cuts, that's going to have to be something we look at as a group, keeping the best interests of Dominion first and foremost.

"Let me be clear. I do not blame you or your staff for the MRSA problem or the attrition increase. And while Bob and Henry might have more to do with these problems than they realize, I don't blame them, either. As I've been saying, there's a fundamental people problem at Dominion, which is why I brought in the consultants and am trying to build a constituency for change—and that change will include us all.

The Third Domain of Organizational Excellence

"So, Debbie, I am asking you, in our executive team meetings, to speak clearly to the needs of your nurses and the hospital as a whole. I am asking everyone, including Sally and Julie, to be constructive, undaunted, and proactive in shaping the future of Dominion."

Debbie looked thoughtful, mulling over what Charlie had just said. "I'll give it a shot," she said finally. "As long as we all get to contribute our ideas, I'm willing."

"Good," Charlie said. "Then I'll be counting on you at the executive meeting on Friday."

Growth and the Parental Role of Leaders

Right before the team meeting on Friday, Charlie met with Tom and Lee in his office. Charlie brought the two consultants up to speed on his latest round of observations. "Summing it all up, I would say that there are two main points. First, we've cut back on training across the board, limiting our opportunity to hone the technical skills of our employees; we've applied the cut-backs selectively, creating winners and losers; and we've never devoted a cent, as far as I can tell, to training that addresses the people side of business. Second, we're hardly making the most of the skills our people have. Too many Dominion employees at all levels of the company feel that their contributions are not valued. In fact, as in the case of Dan Welch in billing and Debbie Smith, our nursing director, they've been at best ignored and at worst discouraged."

"That's a fair appraisal," said Tom, looking up from his notes. "It sounds bleak, but the upside is that you have a much better handle on the problem than you did before. And you've found many sincere, hard-working people at Dominion who would contribute in the right circumstances."

"I think that's true," Charlie said, "but the one thing that still bothers me, although I didn't mention it to her at the time, was Debbie's assumption that I was just like Bob and Henry and committed to continuing their policies."

Lee didn't hesitate. "I think Debbie's assumptions were perfectly reasonable," he said.

"You do?" said Charlie, surprised.

"Absolutely. How was Debbie to know differently?" Lee went on. "You only reached out to her this week. You've been CEO for four months now. How was she supposed to know your ideas were different from Bob's?"

"I suppose that's right," Charlie admitted.

"Remind you of anyone?" Lee asked.

It was a second before it came to Charlie. "You're talking about the business with Ryan and Joyce, the nurse who filed the grievance." Charlie said. "He too needed to address her emotions."

"That's right," Lee replied. "But to be fair, Debbie's reaction was complicated by the dynamics that exist between the sexes in any institution. Some of them are cultural, some of them are sexual, and some of them come out of the family issues that we've been talking about."

"You mean the idea that people naturally think about male leaders as fathers," Charlie said.

"You've got it," said Tom. "Take Jim's approach to leadership. He was paternalistic and sexist, but because he was kind, supportive, and caring, like a good father, Debbie was devoted to him. However, the bottom line was that he provided nurses with training because he saw it as an essential element of his campaign to turn Dominion into a first-class health system. That was his life's work.

"Bob has many of the same attitudes about women, but he lacks the vision and the human touch that made those attitudes palatable when Jim adopted them. Take his approach to the executive team: Bob viewed the team in terms of their ability to achieve specific financial and quality goals. He asked them to leap through a series of hoops, and he did so without recognizing their efforts or providing the least bit of encouragement. As a parent figure, he was aloof and mostly absent, but when he was present, he bestowed his attentions unevenly and unfairly, creating anger and resentment. Barry got extension after extension on his EMR project, while Sally had her training budget cut and Debbie got the bulk of the blame for the MRSA outbreak.

"In the final analysis," Tom said. "Neither Jim nor Bob attended to the need for the executive team members to develop their own leadership skills. To put it another way, as parents, they showed no interest in helping their children grow up, in providing the guidance that would help them mature."

"I see what you're getting at," Charlie said. "There's a tremendous waste of resources here. Someone like Sally or Julie never has had the opportunity to really blossom."

"Which gets to the heart of our vision of leadership," said Lee. "Because leaders are seen as being parents, their best option is to act like supportive parents, providing the guidance that can bring employees along to the point where they can make their own independent contributions to the team."

The Need for Mastery

"The neat thing about this approach is that it dovetails nicely with another fundamental drive that we all feel, one that parallels the need for attachment," Tom added. "Humans are hard-wired to be curious, to learn new things, and to solve problems; they want to figure out new things. On the job, they look for opportunities for growth so that they can achieve mastery. When they are encouraged to contribute to the company, it helps them feel valued personally and as a member of the team. This is exactly what Dan Welch in billing is looking for.

"Our ancestors survived and flourished in harsh environments not simply because they had reasoning skills, but because they found satisfaction in using them. Puzzles attract people, because they enjoy proving that they can master and manage their surroundings. It's no surprise that research consistently identifies the attainment of mastery as the most important source of job satisfaction."

"This fits in with Debbie's point that the motivating force for nurses is the opportunity to improve their skills," Charlie said.

"That's exactly right," Tom replied. "People want to grow in their jobs and take on new challenges, and they value the kind of guidance a leader can provide in helping them achieve new levels of mastery. This can include everything from the kind of training courses that Sally organizes to mentoring programs to executive education at a university. People seek autonomy to achieve mastery."

"Wait a second," Charlie said. "Isn't too much autonomy the problem I'm having right now? Everyone on my executive team is acting autonomously and going off in separate directions."

"You're right—and that's not what we want to encourage," Lee said. "In psychology, we use *autonomy* in a specialized way. For us, autonomy means that people have the capacity to perform on their own, master information, learn new skills, assess alternatives, and make decisions. Autonomous people exercise control over themselves as well as their environment. They will modify their diets when they learn their food is unhealthy, for instance. They will follow treatment regimens to overcome medical problems. Essentially, you can think of an autonomous person as a grownup.

"People seek autonomy because they want to be able to master their environment on their own. This makes them feel safe, secure, and competent. When they are able to function autonomously, they can progress toward mastery. Feeling confident and competent also makes it easier for people to cooperate with others as part of a team. And being part of a team makes them feel even more safe and secure and competent, which promotes autonomy, which in turn leads to even higher levels of mastery. It's a virtuous cycle."

"Okay, I think I see where you're going," said Charlie thoughtfully, "but clearly this cycle also works in reverse. Part of the problem with the women on my executive team is that they haven't been allowed to act autonomously, which makes them feel less safe, secure, and competent. That's why they have been sticking close to the sidelines."

"Exactly," Lee replied, "but when they have a leader who helps them develop their capacity to act autonomously—something you've been doing quite well—they will start pulling together and working as a team. When autonomous people work for an organization whose values align with theirs, they become a powerful driver of organizational success. Our vision of the perfect team is a group of autonomous thinkers, working together under the guidance of a leader, to achieve mastery over the problems confronting the organization."

Charlie thought a bit about what Tom and Lee were getting at. "So, my job is to present appropriate challenges to the team and to make sure the team addresses those challenges to secure a better future for Dominion."

"That's it in a nutshell," Tom said, looking over his glasses. "I think you've got it. And that brings us back to our first conversation, when we brought up the three domains of expertise required to run a successful organization: the business domain, the technical domain, and the people domain. In each of these areas, you need to decide what specific skills are required and then provide opportunities—training, coaching, executive education, whatever—to help people master them. And while the specific types of knowledge necessary for mastery in the technical and business domains may vary from department to department, the knowledge and skills needed for mastery in the people domain are universal."

"So clearly one of the things I need to think about," Charlie said, "is how leaders at Dominion can master the skills needed to support independent thinking by their team members."

"That's certainly one important step you could take," Tom replied. "I don't know if you remember, but at our first session, we also mentioned our colleague John Pickering and his idea that the network-talent model, rather than a traditional hierarchical model, works best in complex organizations. But his model presupposed autonomous employees. When a patient comes in to the emergency room, a team comes together—crossing many departments of the hospital—to take care of that person. The composition of that team changes, depending on the diagnosis. Sure, the team has a leader, but information is shared widely, everyone on the team plays a role in decision making, and the team adapts rapidly and organically as the situation changes.

"Contrast this to the linear models that Jim and Bob used. Every decision was routed to the top, and executive team members wouldn't act until the CEO told them what to do. Neither of your predecessors engaged the team members' desires for growth and mastery and reconciled them with the interests of the organization. The result was an organization that was underperforming in many ways. Mechanisms for information circulation and problem solving atrophied. And the organization lost access to the ideas and knowledge that could help it reach its full potential."

"This makes sense to me," Charlie said. "At least I think it does, but I wonder if the members of my executive team will see it the same way."

"You can introduce the topic at the executive meeting and see if it flies," Lee said. "In any case, we have to get over to the conference room. The meeting is about to start."

The three men got up and headed out the door. "By the way," Tom said as they passed Charlie's assistant on the way out of the suite, "I really like your roses."

The Executive Team Tackles Staff Development

Charlie noticed as he entered the conference room that people were standing and talking in groups. He couldn't remember the last time he had seen Henry and Julie having an informal conversation, but it looked to him as though they were making up for lost time. Barry was the only person immune to the change in atmosphere. He was looking self-consciously aloof and self-contained. "Well," thought Charlie, "that's his loss." Seeing Charlie step to the head of the table, the team members wound down their conversations and returned to their accustomed seats. Lee and Tom filed to the back of the room.

"Good to see you all," Charlie began. "It was a little more than four weeks ago that we had an emergency meeting to discuss MRSA. I'm told that we have new figures. Ryan and Sally, do you want to fill us in?"

Ryan distributed handouts while Sally glanced over her notes. "While it's too early to say that we have the MRSA infection licked, the numbers haven't gotten worse, and we've taken a number of steps that should make a big difference. The MRSA task force that Ryan and I led has members from across the hospital. We have physicians, nurses, respiratory therapists, social workers, housekeepers—the whole nine yards—on the task force, and seems to have not only added depth to our discussions but also given us a great deal of credibility around the hospital. We've looked at best practices at other hospitals, made the rounds of the different units, and are focused on engaging teams to follow through with the meticulous work necessary to reduce the infection rate. We are confident that task force members will serve as champions for MRSA change in their units."

A few of the executive team members asked questions and made suggestions. Charlie took a moment to comment on the work of the MRSA task force and then moved the conversation along to the next issue on his agenda. "I'm very excited about what Ryan and Sally are doing—and especially the collaboration they've encouraged. I think it sends exactly the right message to our staff, which is that we want to hear their best ideas.

"And that brings me to the next step in my exploration of the people side of business at Dominion. Last week we discussed the need to ensure that people at Dominion feel safe and secure. Among other issues, we touched on providing support for our staff and the relationship between a supported staff and the quality of the care we provide our patients. We also discussed the importance of teaming. All these ideas are an outgrowth of my consultations with Tom and Lee, and my discussions with you are a valuable part of our attempt to learn more about the people side of business at Dominion. Ultimately, we're moving toward creating a shared framework for working with people. For now, I would like to get your feedback on how we support staff development here at Dominion."

"*Staff development?*" asked Henry, jumping right in. "I don't want to be difficult, but how's that different from *training?* Certainly, we have always sent the message to our staff that we support ongoing continuing education whenever we could afford it. Is that what you mean by staff development?"

"Not exactly," Charlie replied. "Training is something people take. Development is something that happens within them. I'm interested in finding out if Dominion has a demonstrated commitment to providing staff the opportunity for growth and mastery on the job. I'd like to find out whether staff members feel challenged, engaged, and fulfilled in their work. And I'm wondering whether we do an effective job of capturing that natural desire to learn and using it for the good of the organization."

"Those are a lot of questions to answer," Henry said stubbornly, and everyone in the room seemed to agree.

After a pause, Debbie spoke up, true to her resolution to continue speaking her mind. "My staff likes to learn, which is why the cuts in the training budget were particularly hard on us. My hope is that we can make a commitment to the fullest development of our staff. At the same time, it makes no sense to get behind staff development and not actually take advantage of the contributions that a more knowledgeable staff can make. To do that, Dominion as an institution has to be open to new perspectives and new ideas. All members of this organization should feel that they can get a hearing for their ideas and suggestions—and that has to start with the executive team." Charlie was impressed. Debbie had seemed to take his assurances to heart.

"Debbie is exactly right," said Julie. "For as long as I've been here, I've felt that marketing is viewed as a sort of third wheel.

The Third Domain of Organizational Excellence

My staff feels isolated, frustrated, and disenfranchised. We are doing the best we can, but we really can't market the hospital effectively unless we are part of the team. For instance, it is very difficult for one of my staff members to get an appointment to talk to doctors about marketing initiatives that will ultimately strengthen their practice."

"Julie is making a very important point," Charlie said. "If we don't acknowledge that other people have competencies in areas that are important to the hospital, we're sending the message that we really don't care about them or the efforts they make to build those competencies."

"If that's the case, then I think we have been undermining mastery here, and we go about it in a variety of ways," Sally said. "Contributions from doctors and administrators are always welcomed; contributions from nurses, sometimes; contributions from nearly everyone else, never. Doctors get all the training they want. Nurses see their training budget cut in the name of fiscal responsibility. Housekeepers, food service personnel, and maintenance staff get virtually no additional training beyond what it takes to do their jobs. Fundamentally, it's a question of whether we value all of our employees. We have a pretty rigid class structure here at Dominion."

Henry threw up his hands, "You know, I agree there is a class system here. But what else is new? Every business I've been associated with has had a class system. I saw the same thing at an engineering firm I worked for. Engineers were the top dogs; everyone else did their bidding. This is simply the way things work in business, and I doubt if we can do anything about it. There is no point in arguing about something you can't change. It's inevitable."

"Well, Henry," Charlie responded, "I don't think this kind of class structure is inevitable unless we decide to permit it, which we won't. It's critical for Dominion's success that all of its staff be able to speak their mind and contribute their perspectives. We may not decide to act on their viewpoints, but at least we will have the benefit of them. And it's equally important that people can raise issues they think will improve the organization. If there are problems, I don't want them swept under the rug. When problems are out in the open, we can address them together.

"And this has to start with the executive team. To succeed, we need a team of contributors at the top, not a collection of competitors. I want an executive team where we consider every member's ideas equally, without reference to rank and title. So, if anyone wants to share ideas or concerns, please, let's hear them!"

The Work-Life Balance

"As an HR professional," Sally said, "I have a concern I'd like to bring up."

"Go right ahead," Charlie said.

"I've just said that physicians and administrators are the privileged class at Dominion," Sally went on. "But there's a flip side to their privilege. We expect them to work as long as necessary to get the job done, and this is particularly true of men. Putting in a 70- or 80-hour week here is nothing special. Their home life suffers and, ultimately, their work suffers. How can you make a sustained contribution if you're exhausted all the time? I wonder how much mastery we feel when our lives are out of balance? One of the items I'd like to put on the table is work-life balance."

Knowing all too well that he was one of the people who put in long hours at the hospital, Bob felt compelled to respond. "Sally, while the work-life balance thing makes good sense in principle, the bottom line is that if we don't spend the time doing the work, this place will not run properly. Furthermore, my kids are grown, I have the time, and working for Dominion is a source of real satisfaction for me. I really don't see why this should become an issue for the executive team."

"It's an issue because not everyone has grown children," Sally replied. "Look, Bob, this is not about you. We all have a tendency to extrapolate from our personal experiences, but we need to think about the hospital as a whole and develop a sound policy that encourages autonomy and creativity, rather than endurance. And it should be flexible enough to reflect different levels of responsibility and individual circumstances."

Bob was willing to find common ground. "Certainly we can all agree that the staff wants to learn and develop their skills, and that we should support them in this effort. And we should welcome their contributions and apply them for the good of the organization. However, I am not ready to add work-life balance to our growing list of priorities."

Charlie jumped in to prevent Bob from digging in. "I respect your reservations about bringing this up, Bob, and I respect your commitment to Dominion. The commitment of people like you is one of the reasons I came here. But commitment doesn't necessarily have to translate into excessive hours all year long. Sure, there are going to be crunch times, but people want to feel mastery at their jobs as well as in their personal lives. To achieve this, they need a balance. My contention is that employees who have their lives in order, who have a work-life balance, are more productive employees."

"That's fair enough," said Bob. "I can see that."

Charlie was feeling pretty good about the meeting so far. It seemed as though the cold war among members of the executive team was beginning to thaw. And the conversation that followed—about restoring some of the cuts to the training budget for the coming fiscal year—found team members speaking frankly and looking for consensus. It was a good sign. Charlie closed the meeting by thanking the team for their constructive participation. The group broke up slowly, as team members followed up among themselves.

Charlie noticed Lee and Tom slipping out the door with their heads together, and wondered what they thought. He said good-bye, and headed back to his office to meet with them.

The Post Meeting Follow-Up on Team Growth

Charlie found Tom and Lee chatting in the waiting room outside his office. He was elated. "Hey, I think something happened during that meeting. That was progress, wasn't it?"

Smiling broadly, Lee shook Charlie's hand. "Congratulations are in order. Your team is starting to come together, and I think everything you've done in the last month is beginning to pay off. You've given team members the support they need to feel safe speaking out, and you've done so without losing your focus on your own objectives. You recognized people's genuine distress and avoided assigning blame. You've even made it possible for Henry and Bob to relax a bit and consider other alternatives to their own viewpoints. What was also great about it was that, with the exception of Barry, all the team members had their say. There were no winners and losers."

"In our view," added Tom, "you did one of the things leaders must do: you created the norms for constructive interactions. At the same time, leaders must also participate as part of the team in defining outcomes for the organization. You did both."

"Thanks very much," replied Charlie. "And I have to tell you, I feel pretty good about what happened in there. But what's up with Barry? As you've said, people want to have the opportunity to grow and to achieve mastery, but I wonder about him. And I wonder if the entire staff wants to grow and change."

"That's a fair question," Tom said. "Look, we believe that there is an intrinsic desire for growth and mastery that everyone shares, but this natural desire may be undermined in people who are afraid of failure and rejection. They opt for a safe and secure method of doing their jobs, and they cling to what they know. We've found that there is much truth to John Maxwell's observation, 'People are more comfortable with old problems than new solutions.' Your responsibility is to create opportunities for growth and mastery and provide your staff with the support they need to take advantage of them. You want to create a culture that encourages the acquisition and integration of new skills. After all, if you're going to define and hold staff accountable for outcomes, it only makes sense that you support the employee growth needed to achieve them.

"But when you begin changing culture, it is hard to know who will blossom and seize the opportunity to grow. Some people will go for it and others won't. As we've said, it is not your job to change the personalities of your employees. You provide the supportive environment and see who responds. Then, of course, you get behind those who do and provide opportunities for their growth. Your other employees will soon notice, and over time you should reach most of them."

"So what do I do about people like Barry, who, for one reason or another, seems to resist the opportunity for growth?" Charlie asked.

"I don't think we know yet," replied Tom. "We need more information. You might want to include a visit to the IT department in your next assessment. It would be worthwhile to know if Barry feels safe. It could be that he feels overwhelmed by the complexity of implementing a hospital-wide electronic medical record system. That's a big undertaking."

"That's true," Lee added. "It's hard to overstate the importance of making people feel safe. Remember Deming's imperative to 'stamp out fear.' Recent research in neuroscience only underscores this point. When people feel safe and seek growth, they release neurotransmitters that improve brain plasticity and produce a sense of well-being. When there is no safety and people do only what they know, these neurotransmitters aren't released and nothing changes.

"As an organization makes it safe to take on challenges, to take the risk of failing, more and more of the staff will seek opportunities for growth. When more of your staff works toward mastery, your organization will be better equipped to achieve its complex mission. In addition to support, your role in the process is to align those opportunities with your goals for the organization. Tom Peters, in his book *In Search of Excellence*, gets at this when he points out the value of aligning the individual's innate desire for mastery with the organization's particular aspirations for excellence."

"So in addition to building a safe and supportive environment for growth," Charlie said, "I also have to shape the opportunities we offer."

"That's right," said Lee. "This means finding opportunities that mesh with your organization's goals. But it also means presenting challenges that are at the right scale. While it may be appealing to push for dramatic, quantum change, these types of challenges can seem intimidating to many people. Pushing too hard, which is what Bob did, can produce resistance and withdrawal because people are frightened by the risk of failure. Incremental change feels safer and more doable. It's important for leaders to realistically assess an individual's capacity for growth, because mastery can only be accomplished within the individual's limits. Some of your best long-term employees will be the ones who grow one small step at a time.

"You also need to actively encourage people to take advantage of these opportunities—"

"You mean through recognition, material support, and promotion?" Charlie interjected, though it wasn't really a question. "I had always thought that rewarding people was simply the right thing to do—and it certainly is—but seen from this point of view, it's more than a quid pro quo. Recognizing mastery is essential to worker satisfaction, and that drives long-term organizational growth."

"That's correct," Lee said. "But to provide rewards, you also have to measure progress. Measurement helps employees know where they stand—People generally like that—while helping employers better understand the capacity of their employees. Measuring growth on an individualized and team basis becomes a significant strategic tool for optimizing the productivity of your workforce. And it's critical to the concept of accountability that we are going to talk about in the coming week."

"This gets me back to the question I asked you before the meeting," Charlie said. "We're talking a lot about individual growth and mastery, but ultimately what we really need at Dominion is strong teams."

"They are interrelated," Tom replied. "If you have team members who are not functioning well individually, then the team as a whole is unlikely to function well. A team is not 'only as strong as its weakest link'; it is only as strong as the collective capabilities of its members. The job of the team leader is to hire the best members, develop their mastery, and encourage synergy in the group process. The ultimate goal is for the entire team, not the leader, to take responsibility for its own mastery and its results."

"Boy, that's where I'd like to be," Charlie said. "The challenge of making change happen on my own is a bit daunting, especially when I'm set on changing the people culture at Dominion."

The Third Domain of Organizational Excellence

"Well, it's starting to happen, Charlie," said Lee. "It really is. What the meeting today demonstrated was that the executive team is beginning to share in the process. They are taking the responsibility for transforming their own culture and bringing each other along. You could see it not only in what they said, but in how they said it. And this team approach will extend to any challenge you bring to them. Ultimately, the executive team will take change for granted, and, over time, change will spread throughout the entire organization. It will not be feared."

Putting Work-Life Balance into Practice

"I have a question about the issue Sally raised, about work-life balance," Charlie said. "What did you think about the position I took? I said that, for me, the real issue is people achieving mastery in their personal lives as well as their work lives."

"I think that's correct," Tom replied. "Companies that make demands of their workers at the expense of family involvement, whatever that is, will pay a price in unhappy and less productive workers. The organization benefits by encouraging growth in the personal lives of its employees, because this will enhance their productivity and sense of well-being. This could take the form of personal days, telecommuting, or life management services that enable people to make the most of their time off."

"Actually we have a good number of these," Charlie noted. "Henry acts like he's touched a live wire whenever we talk about them, as though he sees these programs as expensive luxuries."

"And we see them as investments that prove their worth over time," said Lee, "but you were right to acknowledge that work-life balance means different things to different people. It's complicated. Here's another perspective on Joyce Williams, the nurse in oncology. Like Bob, she has grown children and derived a great deal of satisfaction from working for Dominion. Unlike Bob, though, her commitment to Dominion led her to feel entitled to a promotion, creating some difficulties for the organization and some pain for her. Developing a work-life policy that staff will view as fair and flexible would be a good challenge for Sally. You might think about tasking her with it once the MRSA work begins to show results."

"This is all interrelated, isn't it?" Charlie commented. "I would love to ask a few more questions, but unfortunately I have to run. What would you like for me to look at in the interim before our next meeting?"

"Our fifth principle—*People need structure to shape and motivate their behavior*—focuses on structure and accountability," said Tom. "By this we mean job expectations, and the system of rewards and consequences that reinforces them. Why don't you look at Dominion through those lenses? You might find out if Dominion spells out these rewards and consequences in writing and has them readily available. You might also want to look into what employees think about these standards. See if employees feel the standards are being applied consistently and fairly."

"In other words, do my usual nosing around," said Charlie.

"Exactly," said Tom. "You're really good at it."

The Third Domain of Organizational Excellence

Principle 4: People want an opportunity for growth to achieve mastery

1. People want mastery of their environment. This is a survival instinct, a developmental imperative, and a source of personal satisfaction. To achieve mastery, people want to learn and grow. People prefer to act autonomously and to think independently in their quest for mastery. They want to grow in their jobs and take on new challenges.

2. Safe and supportive environments improve the likelihood of individuals seeking mastery for themselves and the organization. Leadership must model, support, and facilitate growth for the acquisition of mastery. Fear undermines the initiative to seek mastery by making growth seem dangerous. Incremental manageable challenges seem more safe and attainable; they also increase engagement and motivation.

3. People seek mastery in both their personal and professional lives. When they are unable to achieve mastery in their personal lives, their ability to achieve mastery in their professional lives suffers. This makes it imperative for employers to ensure employees have the opportunity to attain a work-life balance.

CHAPTER 5

PEOPLE NEED STRUCTURE TO SHAPE AND MOTIVATE THEIR BEHAVIOR

Charlie hadn't been in his office 10 minutes Monday morning when the phone started ringing. He looked up from his budget review, exasperated. Charlie had asked Bob to get him the numbers on the electronic medical record system project, and he had been hoping to use the hour or so before everyone else arrived to get a sense of how Barry was doing with the project. Exactly what was so important that whoever was on the line couldn't wait until the start of the workday to call? Charlie sighed and reached for the receiver. When he heard the voice on the phone, though, he sat up a little straighter in his chair and listened attentively. He nodded a few times and hung up. "Well," he thought, "the week is not exactly getting off to a great start."

Sally walked through the door 30 minutes later. "So, we have a highly temperamental surgeon on our hands," Charlie remarked, and Sally nodded grimly.

"I'm really sorry to disturb you, but I felt I could use your help, because it involves some of our senior management," Sally said. "And I knew it might be hard to get some time with you later today," she continued, gesturing at the piles of printouts on his desk.

"That's okay," Charlie replied. "From what you said on the phone, I'm glad you came in. Tell me again what happened. You got a call yesterday afternoon from an operating room nurse?"

"That's right. Nurse Shannon Heinzmann called and was quite upset. She's an experienced OR nurse, and she's very well respected, but she's had to bear the brunt of yet another outburst by Mark Bartholomew—He's one of the surgeons that Lou Perrott, the head of surgery, hired as part of Jim's campaign to make Dominion a force to be reckoned with—and it was evidently the last straw."

"You say he threw a scalpel on the floor and yelled at her because she gave him the wrong instrument? In the OR? With a patient on the operating table? That's really not acceptable."

"Maybe it's not acceptable, but if what she says is true, it's not that unusual. This is the fifth time in the last two months that he's thrown instruments and yelled at her—though this is the first time he's thrown anything as dangerous as a scalpel. She maintains that she gives him the instruments according to the surgical plan, but at some point in the operation he changes his mind—and somehow expects her to intuit the change."

"The episode itself is just part of the problem, isn't it? You said she's complained to Debbie a number of times, but nothing happened."

"Well, not exactly nothing, but close to it. Shannon said she talked to Debbie after the first incident. She was taken aback to find Debbie making excuses for Mark rather than supporting her. 'He's under a lot of pressure,' Debbie told her. 'He and his wife have separated; he's had to move out.' In any case, Debbie urged Shannon to be more sympathetic and to give Dr. Bartholomew some space."

"Let's see. We have a surgeon throwing temper tantrums in the OR, and Debbie, the director of nursing, isn't doing anything to support a member of her team," said Charlie in amazement.

"After a few more incidents, Shannon ran out of patience and complained to Debbie again, who finally talked to Lou. Lou told Debbie he'd talk to Mark and see if he could get him to calm down, but whatever Lou said to Mark—if he did talk to

Mark—didn't have much impact. When Mark threw a scalpel last Friday, Shannon went to Debbie again, but Debbie essentially told her that, while she agreed with her that Mark's behavior was inexcusable, she had done all she could. Shannon was shocked, but what really infuriated her was that Debbie couldn't tell her if Lou had actually talked to Mark or not. It appears that Debbie has never followed up.

"So, after stewing most of the weekend, Shannon called me at home yesterday afternoon. She absolutely refuses to work with Mark again, she's angry with Debbie, and she's considering filing a grievance. She told me she's started looking for a new job, but I think she called because she would rather have something done about the problem than leave."

"And I appreciate that," said Charlie. "She hasn't been treated fairly, and no one—not even the director of nursing—supported her, but she still feels enough loyalty to Dominion not to walk away. And clearly Mark feels no sense of accountability toward anyone," Charlie added, thinking about the issues Tom and Lee asked him to track this week. "What do you know about him?"

"I did some discreet calling around after Shannon phoned," said Sally. "Mark is evidently highly regarded as a surgeon and a top revenue producer for the department. His results are generally quite good, and patients are well satisfied with his work. Not surprisingly, though, the nursing staff didn't like him very much even before he started throwing instruments. One nurse told me he is arrogant, impatient, and condescending—and that he has humiliated a number of other nurses in the last few months."

"So what's our plan?" asked Charlie.

"I think we have to deal with the immediate problem: holding Mark accountable for his actions. He's been disrespectful to another professional, he's jeopardized his colleagues and his patients, and he's created a situation that could pose a real threat to the hospital." Sally knew the decision was Charlie's to make.

"All true. And we have to somehow work with Lou and Debbie so that they start holding members of their teams accountable," Charlie added. "If they had done their jobs, neither one of us would have needed to get involved in this. On the other hand, this is just another instance of the double standard you were talking about at the executive team meeting, and that's an issue that we all need to address. If a nurse threw a tantrum in the OR, I doubt if Lou would have asked his surgeons to be sympathetic. This kind of thinking is so deeply ingrained that Debbie, of all people, subscribes to it. It's amazing!

"The first thing to do will be for me to meet with Lou and Debbie," Charlie continued, standing up and walking with Sally into his outer office, where his assistant was getting settled for the day. "I need to find out more about what's keeping them from holding Mark accountable and supporting Shannon— and then work out a plan with them to make sure they do both. And because Shannon called you, I think you should follow up with her and give her a general sense of what's going on. You don't have to be too detailed, but let's see if we can find a way to restore her faith in Dominion."

After Sally left, his assistant turned to Charlie and asked him how his weekend had gone. "It was pretty nice," Charlie said,

The Third Domain of Organizational Excellence

"but it's definitely over. I'd like to see Lou and Debbie this afternoon. Would you set it up? Tell them I'd like to talk about Mark Bartholomew. And let's meet in Debbie's office."

Charlie Insists on Accountability

At three, Charlie walked over to Debbie's office, which he couldn't help but noticing had a view of the hospital's meditation garden rather than the parking lot. Although it was spacious and well lit, the room was hardly restful and calm. It seemed to be overflowing with paper. There were stacks of paper everywhere, on top of file cabinets, leaning against the walls, and scattered across Debbie's desk.

"Sorry about the mess," Debbie said while she cleared the top of her conference table and dumped the journals she had been storing on her conference chairs on the floor so that Charlie could sit down. "I have been meaning to do something about it, but I never seem to find the time."

"I guess you don't have conferences here very often," Charlie observed.

"Hardly ever," Debbie replied a little evasively. "It's easier for me to get out and talk to the nurses one on one." She stopped talking abruptly when Lou entered the room. Lou had left his harpoon on the wall of his office, but you wouldn't have guessed it from the expression on Debbie's face. Her face took on a hunted, vigilant look, while Lou, for his part, looked like he hadn't a care in the world. Clearly, he wasn't worried about the meeting.

The three of them stood there for a second, and when it became apparent that Debbie wasn't going to say anything more, Charlie asked them both to sit down. "Sally has had a serious complaint from one of the nurses about Dr. Bartholomew's tantrums in the OR," said Charlie. "He's been throwing instruments and yelling at nurses. And on Friday, he let loose with a scalpel. He could have injured someone."

"You're a doctor," Lou said, nonchalantly. "You know surgeons. They're prima donnas; that's just the way it is. It takes a person with a certain amount of ego to be a surgeon. You just have to accept the whole package."

While Lou was speaking, Charlie thought about Henry's comments about the engineering firm he used to work for. Both men would rather accept a dysfunctional hierarchy than change.

"Besides, given what I know about Mark's personal life, I'm not surprised," Lou went on. "He's under a lot of pressure."

"Pressure?" Debbie asked incredulously. "Pressure? What do you think that scrub nurse felt after Dr. Bartholomew humiliated her? She had to keep her focus on the operation despite how upset she was. It's just not right."

Lou looked puzzled. "When we had our discussion about Mark, you certainly didn't take that tone with me," he said. "I thought we both agreed that Mark had a lot on his plate these days, with his separation and all, and that I would just talk to him."

"So what happened?" Charlie asked, trying to head off a dispute.

"Well, I talked to him," Lou said, "but I could tell he was just listening politely. As far as he's concerned, surgeons are in charge in the operating room, and he doesn't think they should be second-guessed. Besides, he thinks he can go anywhere he wants because he is such a successful surgeon. He's probably right, you know. He would be a good find for any hospital."

"Did you get back to Debbie about your conversation?" Charlie asked.

"I have a busy surgery department to run, and Mark's behavior in the operating room hasn't interfered with his results," Lou said. After a pause, he added, "And frankly it never occurred to me."

Charlie turned to Debbie. "And you never followed up with Lou?"

"I felt I had done all I could," said Debbie. "Besides, I've had these conversations with doctors before, and they never go anywhere. They blame us for anything that goes wrong at the hospital, whether it's the wrong instrument or the MRSA outbreak. They certainly never support us. And of course, they can get away with throwing contaminated instruments."

Charlie knew that Debbie had a legitimate complaint, but it seemed to him that she was using it as an excuse not to follow through. "And what about getting back to Shannon, at least to let her know you talked with Lou?"

"I intended to talk to her next time I ran into her," Debbie said sullenly, "but I've just been so busy."

Charlie looked thoughtfully at both of them for a second, organizing his thoughts. He knew that there was no difference between the hospital and any other business where professionals with seniority feel that the principles of fairness and best practices don't apply to them. The surgeon's behavior was simply unacceptable, regardless of his standing or success. But he also had Debbie and Lou's behavior to contend with.

"The way I see it," Charlie said, "there are two problems here. The first is that no one is holding Mark accountable for his behavior. The second is that because there is no accountability, our teams are not working nearly as well as they should.

"I don't care how talented a surgeon Mark is. He is part of this organization, not an independent operator. Just like everyone else here, he is accountable not simply for his performance but also his behavior. There are no exceptions.

"Think of it this way. We have rules and structure to ensure that everyone works as productively as possible for the good of the hospital. We must apply those rules fairly and universally if everyone here is to perform efficiently. The surgeons need the nurses to follow procedure, and the nurses need the surgeons to lead in a respectful manner. Debbie is right; it's a miracle that Shannon performed so well after Mark humiliated her, but I would guess that she was more than a bit distracted, especially because she felt that Mark would get away with his behavior.

"I'm not willing to accept substandard performance for any reason, and the only way we're going to maximize performance is when all members of the team feel they are accountable for their actions, nurses and surgeons alike. In this case, Mark has not been held accountable. What makes it worse is that, as the leader of the operating room team, Mark is responsible for supporting his team members, not humiliating them.

"So I want both of you to work out a plan to talk to Mark. You must make it clear to him that you will not tolerate further tantrums. You should explain the rationale behind your reasoning and make your expectations of change absolutely clear. At the same time, I'd like you to acknowledge that he's been having some trouble with his home life, and indicate that you want to be personally supportive of him. Are you both on board?"

The two were silent. "I'm not sure why I need to be part of this," Debbie protested.

Charlie thought about how he could phrase his point in a way that would make sense to her. "In our conversations these past few weeks, you've objected that there are separate standards for doctors and nurses at Dominion, and I think you're right. But the reason they need to have the same standard goes back to teaming. You can't have a productive team when some members are held accountable while the others are not. I can't think of a more effective way to show that accountability is not a doctor's issue or a nurse's issue, but a team issue, than for you and Lou to talk to Mark together."

"I don't know how much good it's going to do, but if you want us to talk to Mark, I'm willing," Lou said, though he didn't seem particularly enthusiastic. "I can't guarantee, though, that Mark is going to be very receptive."

"But that's not what I'm asking you to do, Lou," said Charlie. "I'm asking you to set clear limits and to take responsibility for applying them fairly but firmly. Mark's response is out of your control. We could very well lose him, but I'm willing to take that risk. He's likely to resist changing and will need continued coaching, which is your responsibility as well. There may be some grousing from your other surgeons if they hear the story, but you must make it clear that fairness requires that everyone be accountable, as individuals and as part of the team, for their actions."

Lou looked a bit less complacent.

"And that goes for nurses as well as surgeons," Charlie continued, "so in addition to talking to Mark, I'd like for you two to come up with a plan that focuses on strengthening the surgical teams. Get back to me next week and let me know how things are progressing. If you need some guidance, you should talk to Sally. Are we agreed?"

They both nodded glumly. Charlie looked at each of them, stood up, and strode out of the room, leaving the two staring at each other, wondering where to start.

A Contrast in Leadership Styles

As he headed back to his office, Charlie thought about the conversation with Debbie and Lou. He hoped they would rise to the occasion, but he was not entirely confident that they would succeed. Right now, neither was a very effective leader or even much of a team player. Lou took a hands-off approach, letting his surgeons go their own ways. Debbie's strategy, if you could call it that, was to try to cultivate individual relationships with her staff, with the result that she lost sight of the big picture and was constantly overwhelmed. It was not surprising, given the disorder of her office, that she had not followed up with Lou or gotten back to Shannon. When it came down to it, neither of them had much of a structured style of leadership.

Charlie wasn't sure that Lou understood the need to impose structure and accountability, just as he failed to concern himself with providing support to his staff. After all, surgery had been a consistent moneymaker for the hospital. Why meddle with a good thing? The issue with Debbie was different. She wanted other people to stop blaming nurses for hospital-wide problems like MRSA, but she didn't seem ready to impose a system of accountability herself.

Charlie was still thinking about Lou and Debbie when he rounded a corner and bumped right into Julie Martinez, knocking the folders she had been carrying to the floor. Apologizing, he dropped to his knees, scooped them up, and handled them back to her. He hadn't had an extended conversation with Julie since their talk in his office two weeks ago, and it occurred to him that he might use the occasion to follow up. "If you're heading back to your office, Julie, I could tag along," he said. "I don't think I've had the chance yet to see the marketing suite."

"As a matter of fact, that's where I'm going," Julie replied. "We have a team meeting in a half hour. I have a few last-minute preparations to make, but I'd be happy to show you around and talk on the way."

"Great," Charlie said. "Are you still feeling like you're working at A&P, not Kroger?" he asked, picking up on the comment she had made during their first extended conversation.

"It's probably too early to draw a conclusion," she said with a smile. "I do think things are starting to change a bit here," Julie said. "I appreciated the opportunity at last week's staff meeting to talk about the isolation and frustration our team feels. It was good to get it out into the open."

"So your team's morale is really suffering?" Charlie inquired.

"Yes and no," Julie said. "It's frustrating when you feel that there is a lot more you can do, but we're all so focused on achieving what we can achieve within the limitations that Jim and Bob created for us that there's not a lot of time for grousing. I'm lucky in that I have a very good team, with many talented people. I think they stay because they like working with each other, and they respect each other."

Julie and Charlie had entered the marketing suite. "Let me introduce you to a few of the people who get the good word out about Dominion," Julie said as she walked with him down a central corridor lined with framed award certificates and copies of Dominion's latest ad campaign. All the doors along the hallway were open, and Julie knocked on doorframes and introduced Charlie as they worked their way down to a large room at the end. "We put the writers and our account executives in rooms of their own," Julie explained. "They need the quiet, and they spend a fair amount of time on phone."

"The designers seem to thrive in an open environment, so we've created a large work space for them," she said, ushering Charlie into a sun-lit room with two designers who were staring intently at oversize monitors. They all seemed pleased to meet

Charlie, but they all returned to their work as soon as Julie had introduced them to Charlie.

"And this is my office," Julie said, pointing to a small office at the back of the large room. I have a window in the wall overlooking the graphics area, so people can see what I'm up to, but I can close the blinds if I need to really focus."

Charlie couldn't help contrasting Julie's approach with Henry's. Like Henry, she wanted the members of her staff to have a nice work environment, but instead of treating them as if they were indistinguishable, she had designed the marketing suite so that each person would have a workspace suitable to his or her needs. And all staff members looked out on a common space; they weren't isolated.

Outside Julie's office, Charlie noticed a large chart that depicted the department's workflow. "I want everyone to know what the team has on its agenda and what they're responsible for individually," Julie explained. "Having the chart in such a visible place helps them figure out what they're accountable for. And we hold all our team meetings at that table in the corner with a clear view of the chart. We're always trying to figure out how to weave new assignments into our existing workflow."

"That's a neat system," Charlie said, as he looked down at his watch, "but I'm worried you've already given me more time than you could spare, especially with a team meeting in a few minutes. But I do have something extra I need for you to try to fit into that workflow. I'd like you to come up with a new marketing plan for Dominion and run it by me in three weeks. I asked Henry to start looking at next year's budget—and I think it's time to reexamine our priorities. Is that possible?"

"Let me talk to the team, and I'll get back to you," Julie said, breaking into a smile. "I don't think there will be any problem, but I just want to make sure that I'm not missing anything."

"Fair enough," said Charlie.

As he returned to the main corridor, Charlie thought about the day. It had started with him puzzling over the EMR project. To be honest he hadn't given it a moment's thought since then, so it was back on top of the agenda for tomorrow morning. But while he was at it, he might as well check in on Barry's IT group, as it was just down the hall.

As he approached the IT office, Charlie noted something odd. Someone had taped a sheet of brown paper to the back of the glass door at the entrance to Dominion's IT department so you couldn't see through it. "That's not especially inviting," Charlie thought. He considered knocking, but decided just to walk in. He found himself in a little reception area with a few empty chairs and a desk in one corner. There was no one there.

He walked through a door on the other side of the desk and down a short corridor. He passed a few offices that looked occupied, but no one seemed to be around. This was a little strange. "Anybody home?" Charlie asked. He heard the sound of a swivel chair sliding across the linoleum and a short, balding man stuck his head into the hallway.

"Can I help you?"

The Third Domain of Organizational Excellence

"I'm looking for Barry Johnson," Charlie said. "Is he around?"

"Nope. He and the rest of the staff went to EMR training, and they left me to hold the fort. They'll be back tomorrow. My name's Jack Farina."

"The entire IT staff is out of the building, and they've left you alone?" Charlie asked. This didn't seem to make much sense.

"That's the extent of it," Jack said. "We're really not at the stage where the EMR program is ready, but Barry wanted the staff to take a look at what we have so far."

"I see," said Charlie noncommittally. This wasn't good either. "Hey, did you ever get a work order to talk to a nurse in pediatrics about modifying the program she uses to process blood samples?"

There was a short pause as the balding man scratched his head. "I think Barry did pass something like that on to me a few weeks ago. It's around here somewhere. He said to get to it when I had a spare moment, but it's been pretty busy here."

"I see," said Charlie, looking down the empty corridor.

"Are you in pediatrics too?" the little man asked. Clearly, Charlie realized, he hadn't even recognized him.

"When Barry comes back, tell him Charlie Fisher was looking for him, okay?"

Charlie watched as recognition finally dawned on Jack, and then turned around and headed out of the office. Barry was running the IT department as if it were barely a part of Dominion. What was worse, he was not on top of the delays in the EMR implementation. Regardless of what the numbers would tell him tomorrow morning, this was a problem he needed to address—and soon.

Charlie Grapples with Accountability and Structure

As Charlie had foreseen, it was a busy week. Nonetheless, he kept coming back to the issue of accountability and the need for structure. He had taken an unequivocal position with Lou and Debbie about holding Mark accountable for his behavior and, furthermore, he had made it clear to them that he held them accountable for their performance as leaders. Intellectually, he knew that holding people accountable for fulfilling their responsibilities was necessary, but he wondered if holding people accountable would detract from the supportive environment he was trying to create. He had told Lou and Debbie that they should acknowledge that Mark was going through a difficult time even as they held him accountable for his behavior in the OR. Could you really hold someone accountable and provide support at the same time? Perhaps Bob was right after all. Maybe he could just do one or the other.

He had another question as well. Mark had clearly violated the rules that governed behavior in the OR, rules designed to protect patients and enhance teamwork and productivity. He had no qualms about holding Mark accountable, but he worried that he was holding Lou and Debbie to standards that had not been clear to them. His expectations were very different from Jim's or Bob's, and so were the processes and structures that he favored. Was he being fair? These were all issues he was anxious to raise with Tom and Lee.

When the two consultants arrived for their Friday appointment, Charlie impatiently led them into his office. "You two are really going to earn your keep today," he remarked before launching into his account of Sally's early-morning call, his subsequent discussion with Lou and Debbie about Mark, and his visits to Julie's and Barry's offices.

"This whole issue of accountability is a tough one for me," he said. "I'm clear in my mind that I needed to hold Mark, Lou, and Debbie accountable, but I don't want to come off like Bob. I certainly don't want to risk losing the supportive environment we've been trying to put in place these last few weeks, and I don't want to create a backlash.

"And interestingly enough, with all of Bob's talk about accountability, I can only say that I've encountered a vacuum of accountability at Dominion, particularly in addressing the people side of business. It's apparent that as long as Lou and Debbie didn't make any waves—as long as they produced numbers that Bob could measure—they weren't held accountable for their leadership."

Lee and Tom looked at each other. They had reached a critical point in Charlie's understanding of their framework. Lee took the lead. "I think you took the only possible position," Lee said. "There's no doubt that holding people accountable can cause discomfort and generate resistance. That said, failure to set limits and impose structure will inevitably undermine the capacity of your organization to achieve peak performance. If it makes you feel better, our experience is that over time the majority of staff will feel more comfortable working in a clearly structured environment, even if the structure is new to them. People like a fair system that is predictable and effective. They like structure."

"Are you going to tell me that the need for structure, like the need for support, has origins in our evolution?" Charlie asked.

"I am," said Lee. "Survival depends on people working together, and structure is the framework of rules and processes necessary for them to act as a cohesive unit. An organization with structure is dynamic and cohesive. It grows by making opportunities happen. An organization without structure is disorganized and falls apart. It lacks a unifying purpose, efficient processes, and misses opportunities."

The Synergy between Support and Accountability

Tom picked up the thread. "You've been talking about accountability and structure as if they are the opposite of support and nurturance. From an organizational point of view, structure serves the same goals as support. Boundaries liberate as well as limit. When you're clear about limits, you define the arena where the individual is free to act, explore, and become creative. Clarity of structure helps people become more secure and autonomous in their roles—and autonomous people, as we've said, are free to apply their best emotional and rational thinking to solving organizational problems. In fact, a safe and supportive environment can only exist when an organization provides clear limits and accountability."

"But Bob insisted on structure and accountability," Charlie objected. "When he took over, he instituted structure, held people accountable for performance, and met with a lot of resistance. I don't want that to happen to me."

"There are a number of differences between your approach and Bob's," Tom replied. "First, Bob's notion of accountability, as you've rightly noted, didn't extend to the people side of business. You're taking a broader view and holding people accountable for creating a safe and secure environment.

"And this gets us to the second difference. As a leader, Bob instituted structure and accountability without himself adhering to the first four principles. He fell into the trap of negative accountability. He responded punitively when people fell short. Rather than rewarding people when they reached his goals or exceeded them, he simply set the bar higher. This provoked resentment and anger among his best performers, causing some of them to start looking elsewhere. People need a meaningful reward system that systematically reinforces the genuine creativity, initiative, and cooperation needed to attain organizational goals. The rewards could range from bonuses to a simple pat on the back. When people get the rewards they deserve, they feel affirmed by the organization, more connected to the enterprise, and motivated to give their best.

"Do you remember what you told us about your conversation with Andy Benjamin, your head of orthopedics? He couldn't recall if he had ever brought his whole team together to recognize the accomplishments of nurses and technicians. Like Lou Perrott, he just assumes that caring for patients is its own reward and has left it at that."

"You know, Charlie," Lee added, "you just can't overestimate the value of active affirmation and recognition. People respond very powerfully when someone important compliments their work or even shows an interest. Think about your encounter with Dan in billing. He really appreciated your stopping by, and he responded by giving frank, helpful answers to your questions. In a similar way, when you implement structure—set rules and expectations—in a positive fashion, people respond favorably. It's easier for them to internalize it, to make it their own. It's important that your managers set high standards, while praising people for their good work, rather than just criticizing them when they fall short. In fact, this idea is particularly important for your male leaders, who are prone to negative feedback and micromanaging."

"Like Bob?" Charlie asked.

"Even Bob would admit he's guilty as charged," said Lee. "I have to add that there is scientific support for this whole discussion. Behavioral psychologists have proven positive reinforcement increases the frequency of behavior, while negative reinforcement decreases them."

"So, your principles don't make behaviorism obsolete," Charlie said remembering his college psychology.

"That's right. Our principles also tie directly to the literature on self-esteem: self-esteem increases when people achieve success within a structure that they understand. This is one of the reasons why employee engagement is so important."

The Third Domain of Organizational Excellence

"Okay, this is all very helpful to me," Charlie said. "As I realized when thinking about my expectations of Lou and Debbie, our work together involves establishing a different kind of structure at Dominion, so I have to be positive about implementing it. Anything else I need to keep in mind?"

"Here's another point," Tom added. "You must apply structure universally and in an impersonal, across-the-board manner for optimal effect. When a rule applies to everyone, people are more likely to accept it, even if it requires them to change their behavior pretty dramatically. And it should be apparent to everyone how these rules promote the success of the organization. When people understand that following a rule contributes in some way to strengthening their organization, they are more likely to follow it.

"On the other hand, it's important to bear in mind that structure is more than rules; it's the culture of the organization, an unspoken code that governs the way people interact. We absorb some of this structure rationally—by learning the rules—but we also absorb it automatically in the subcortical areas of the brain, those more primitive parts of the brain we discussed at lunch a few weeks ago. Managers can and should explain expectations and goals rationally, but employees will get a sense of the overall structure naturally and effortlessly just by operating within it. This creates a challenge for managers. They have to make absolutely sure that all the messages about structure—the ones employees absorb rationally and the ones they absorb unconsciously—are consistent. Managers have to walk the walk as well as talk the talk. If the messages are consistent, employees develop clarity on what they must do to exceed expectations and why.

"It's no wonder that surgical nurses are treated as second-class citizens at Dominion" Tom went on. "Although Lou Perrott told you that his staff was united in providing the best possible care possible, he defined his job as giving his surgeons, more than any other group, the tools they needed to do that. And Andy Benjamin in orthopedics as good as told you that he never gave a thought as to whether nurses felt part of his team."

Charlie looked at his watch. "I hate to stop the conversation, but it's almost time for the meeting, and we haven't touched on how we are going to approach it. Maybe we should just take a moment now and continue the discussion later."

"Good idea," Lee said, "What's on the agenda?"

"There are a number of items. Among others, Bob is scheduled to give a brief overview of the hospital's performance," Charlie replied. "That might provide an opening to talk about structure and accountability with the team."

"I agree," Tom said. "In any case, let's see how the meeting evolves. They are certainly becoming more productive every week."

Bob Reports on Performance

When Charlie entered the room with Tom and Lee, he once again noted with satisfaction that a series of lively conversations were going on around the conference table. Henry was enthusiastically expounding on his plans to spend the weekend playing golf at a resort in South Carolina, and it was clear from what Julie was telling him that she had played there herself. "That's a surprise," thought Charlie. He didn't think Julie was the golf type, but live and learn. Only Barry and Debbie were missing. Charlie assumed Barry was still away at his training session, but he didn't know where Debbie was. As it turned out, she slipped into the room just as he called the meeting to order.

As the executive team went through the agenda, reviewing plans to renovate one of the intensive care units and to open a clinic in a nearby suburb, Charlie was gratified to see almost everyone pitching in with constructive comments. The only exception was Debbie. Though she made a few suggestions about the need for a sleeping bench for family members in the ICU rooms, Debbie was quieter than she had been. Clearly, Charlie realized, she took his reaction to her handling of Lou and Mark as a rebuke—and it certainly was from a professional point of view—but evidently she took it personally, as if from a parent. He made a note to reassure her of his support.

Bob concluded the agenda with a brief overview of the hospital's performance. Although the hospital was operating in the black, profit was down from previous years. Recently, however, utilization rates had stabilized, an encouraging sign.

"As Ryan and Sally noted last week, we seem to be getting a grip on the MRSA problem, although it's too early to know for sure," Bob said. "As far as the hospital's finances are concerned, we have to be very careful if we are to turn our numbers around, especially in this economy."

Bob started punctuating his remarks by jabbing his forefinger on the table. "We have to hold the line," he said, "focusing on quality care, high utilization rates, and careful cost management. If we are going to make progress on these issues, each of you must hold your staff accountable to our policies and benchmarks. When we don't meet our strategic goals, there will be consequences."

The team looked taken aback by Bob's summary, which seemed like a return to the days when Bob was interim CEO. But this time, the silence didn't last long. Sally spoke up. Rather than react defensively, she seemed to be searching for common ground. "I agree that accountability is essential," she said. "As the vice president for human relations, I enforce hospital policy routinely, but I've found that it's really about *how* you hold staff accountable that makes a difference."

Some heads started nodding. "I too completely agree that accountability is essential to our success," said Charlie, joining the discussion. "Bob is right in reminding us of this critical point. But people need to be held accountable for the people side of business as well as the business and technical domains. In addition, accountability must be complemented by acceptance, nurturance, family, and development. In my view, we can only attain peak performance when we have a balance of structure and support."

Defining Structure

"I understand support," Ryan said, clearly thinking about his brush with the grievance process, "but the notion of structure seems to mean different things to different people. What do you mean by *structure*?" he asked Charlie.

"Well, structure is a lot of things," Charlie responded. "It's more than our rules, policies, and procedures. It involves clearly defined roles and expectations of performance. And it includes systematic rewards for success and consequences for failure. It is a mechanism for continuous feedback. Take all these things together, and structure can be seen as the part of our organizational culture that helps us keep on track to achieve our goals."

Debbie felt the need to add, "When the MRSA problem emerged, I felt the structure of accountability, but not the support. If I could have told my staff that the leadership team was behind them in fixing this problem, it would have been a great help to their morale and performance."

"From the point of view of marketing, it seems to me that structure is related to our brand," Julie observed. "In a sense, branding is about defining ourselves and our aspirations. It means we consistently deliver on our promise of quality care."

Charlie was surprised to find Henry nodding his head in agreement and looked at him quizzically. Henry noticed the glance. "You know, Charlie, no one is more surprised than I am that these conversations are beginning to make sense," Henry confessed. "I had been worried that the hospital was moving in a touchy-feely direction and leaving common sense and brass tacks behind, but now I see that support and structure are mutually reinforcing and not opposites. We need both to attain the kind of quality Bob would like to see here."

Sally was about to add something when Charlie looked at his watch. "Look people, our time is up, but feel free to continue this discussion. I'd like for you to start thinking about how we can implement this balance of support and accountability at Dominion. See you next week, if not sooner."

Examining Strategic Planning, Accountability, and Communication

When Tom and Lee caught up with Charlie back at his office, he had a broad grin on his face. "If I say so myself, that's another meeting that went very well."

"We're clearly making progress," Lee said. "With the exception of Debbie, people don't seem angry or defensive."

"I think you're right, although Debbie remains a bit of a puzzle for me," Charlie replied. "I'm not sure what's going on with her."

"It's too early to see yet whether she rises to the challenge you're giving her or retreats into her old habits," observed Tom. "We'll need to see how it evolves."

"And what did you say to Julie when you dropped in on her?" Lee asked. "It must have been terribly motivating. She was more involved in the discussion than I've ever seen her, and I thought her comment about brands and structure was very perceptive."

"So did I," Charlie said. "It helped to visit her office. I certainly was impressed by how she uses structure to motivate and unify her team. That simple workflow chart was in its own modest way a tremendous advantage. It keeps everyone on her team focused on outcomes and allows them to celebrate their accomplishments."

"Before the meeting, we were talking about applying structure in general terms and highlighting the importance of consistency and fairness," Tom added. "Julie's workflow chart suggests that there are other devices and processes you can use to heighten awareness of structure and even to change structure. One of them is the strategic plan. When you have a strategic plan, people understand your organizational goals, how you're going to achieve them, and how their success will be measured. It's motivating."

"This all ties in to our discussion of mastery, doesn't it?" asked Charlie. "While you're holding someone accountable, you're also posing a challenge that can help them grow—if you communicate it clearly."

"That's right," said Lee. "But as you've realized, it takes some care to communicate the need for accountability in a supportive way. You have to be purposeful as well as consistent and clear. When you address your employees, they should assume that you have something important to say. At the same time, you have to be inclusive and caring. You should convey the underlying message, 'We are all in this together.' When you adopt a dictatorial tone, as Bob did, however inadvertently, you just encourage resistance. No one even listens to what you have to say."

"Of course, it's essential to create opportunities for employees to communicate with you. It gives people the chance to offer feedback. You could call town hall meetings and even ask staff to have lunch with you. You have to be willing to give people the opportunity to hold you accountable. You have to listen and respond. In the final analysis, you have to set an example."

"I'm very conscious of that," said Charlie. "But this business of being supportive while simultaneously insisting on accountability still seems tricky."

"That's because it's one of the most difficult aspects of leading and managing people," Lee replied. "Striking a balance between nurturance and structure is at the heart of great leadership. You want your staff to know that you care and that they can function like a family, but you do so because as a business leader you know that family-like structures enable people to work comfortably and optimally. But as we've said before, a business is not a family and you're not a father. Each business has a mission and holds people who are part of it accountable for doing their part in realizing this mission. A family rewards you just for being yourself; a business rewards you for your performance.

"In addition, striking that balance is critical for helping people develop their autonomy and personal accountability. As a manager, you're encouraging them to become autonomous through your support and giving them the structure to measure it through your systems of accountability. The realization of their own goals and the goals of the business become intertwined."

Lee took out a piece of paper. "Here," he said, passing it to Charlie. "This is what we mean."

The Third Domain of Organizational Excellence

BALANCE OF SUPPORT AND STRUCTURE

"Even when leaders are focused on the people side of business," Lee continued, "some leaders' personalities favor structure while others favor support. Those leaders who are more exclusively nurturing neglect the counterbalancing force of structure and the guidance it provides. Conversely, people perceive leaders who use structure alone as controlling and constrictive, not inclusive, perhaps even as threatening. These leaders undermine employee engagement. A key to building your leadership is developing the side where you think you are weakest. You have to have both, and they have to be in productive balance."

Charlie looked over the diagram. "I see, you have to be deliberate in maintaining that equilibrium. But it's hard, because I've seen people on my team respond to support and structure in different ways. Debbie craves support, for instance, but resists structure. On the other hand, Henry responds more to structure than support. How can you accommodate different personalities within the framework of support and structure?"

"That's a good question," Tom said, "which, as it turns out, leads to our last principle: *Individuals are different from one another.* Focus your investigations on that during the next week. As you've pointed out, every person on your team is an individual with a unique character. As you work with them next week, think about your responsibility to them as individuals and how you can square that responsibility with your obligations as the leader of this institution. How can you turn these differences into a plus for Dominion?"

"Okay," said Charlie. "I can do that. But I was wondering how long it will be before we start translating these principles into an action plan for the organization?"

"Well, we have one last principle to cover," Tom said, "then I think it might be worthwhile going over them with the entire executive team, so that they can help you develop your plan."

"I could go for that," Charlie replied.

"How about we schedule a full-day retreat with the executive team in two weeks?" Lee said. "We could spend the morning going over the principles and then translate them into their leadership implications in the afternoon. It will allow your team to get on the same page, so you can build the people side of Dominion together."

"Good idea," said Charlie. "I'll send them an e-mail."

The Third Domain of Organizational Excellence

Principle 5: People need structure to shape and motivate their behavior.

1. People need structure to function effectively in the work environment. Structure consists of such tangible factors as rules, policies, and procedures as well as such intangibles as culture, customs, and traditions that guide people in achieving the organization's goals. Tangible and intangible structure must be consistent, because people both experience structure rationally and assimilate it unconsciously at a deep emotional level.

2. The application of structure must be depersonalized, universal, and predictable for it to have optimal effect. When a leader applies structure this way, it is less likely to be experienced as rejecting.

3. People need clarity about their own accountability to the mission of the organization. When organizations have strategic plans, clearly defined goals, and measures for success, people have clarity about expected outcomes. Individuals and teams perform more effectively when they are in alignment with the rules, values, and goals of the organization.

CHAPTER 6
INDIVIDUALS ARE DIFFERENT FROM ONE ANOTHER

The following week, Charlie hit the ground running. One of the ideas that caught the board's attention when it brought Charlie in for an interview was his assertion that the hospital ought to be reaching out to the affluent, fast-growing suburbs north of town. When the board hired him, it gave him carte blanche to explore the possibilities, and one of the first things he did was to task Bob and Henry with developing a proposal to open a family clinic in the neighborhood. They had been checking the numbers—and they looked promising so far. The three of them spent the entire afternoon on Monday with their real estate consultants, visiting potential sites and discussing their merits.

Tuesday was just as busy. Charlie had a series of meetings with various members of the executive team. Over the course of the day, they developed objectives for a major overhaul of the hospital's website, decided to purchase a powerful MRI to reinforce the hospital's edge in diagnostic imaging, and got a handle on the hospital's staffing needs for the coming year. Charlie was aware that he was not giving as much consideration to the dilemmas of individual differences as he would have liked, but he needn't have worried. On Wednesday, Bob took care of it for him.

Bob called Charlie around nine, asking if he could give him a half hour later in the day to discuss the electronic medical record project. "I have some time around 3:30," Charlie replied. "Would that work?" Bob sounded pretty upset. "I'm not surprised," Charlie thought, thinking about his visit to the IT department the previous week. "I am surprised, though, that it's taken him this long to realize what's happening."

Bob had been sitting impatiently in the outer office for 10 minutes when Charlie came out at 3:30 to bring him back. Charlie could see that Bob was furious. "I gather that things are not going well with the EMR project," Charlie said dryly as they set-tled around his conference table. "How can I help?"

"I went to Barry Johnson's office a few days ago, and that was the last straw," Bob said, trying hard to control his anger. "He's badly mismanaged the EMR project, and, what's worse, he's arrogant and doesn't take direction. I'm not sure even now that I fully understand how bad things are, but the more I uncover, the worse it appears. The constant delays and cost overruns are a drag on our performance. We're devoting a lot of resources to the EMR project, and we're getting precious little for it right now. I didn't see it at the time, but Julie was absolutely correct when she complained a few weeks ago that if she had Barry's budget, she could have a stellar marketing program."

"What's brought things to a head?" Charlie asked.

"Even though Barry reports to me, I've given him a lot of leeway in the last year or so to manage the project on his own," Bob said. "While I was the interim CEO, I had a lot of other issues to worry about, and I thought taking a hands-off approach would be okay since Barry came here with an outstanding résumé."

"What do you mean?"

"When we hired him, Jim and I both thought he was a great find. Before coming here, he had held a series of increas-ingly responsible positions at hospitals around the region. He not only looked good on paper but he also brought with him a convincing vision of what an EMR system could do for Dominion—and it went beyond simply providing dramati-cally more efficient and more effective care for our patients.

He made the case—and quite rightly I thought—that the data we gathered through our EMR system, coupled with sophisticated analytics—would really give us a handle on the health care needs of our population, enabling us to get ahead of the curve and be more proactive."

"There's nothing the matter with that kind of thinking," Charlie agreed, "so what's the problem?"

"The problem," Bob replied, "is that Barry talks a good line, but his follow-through is terrible. In retrospect, all that movement from hospital to hospital should have raised red flags for us."

"Didn't anyone follow up with his previous employers?" Charlie asked.

"Yes, but we could have done a better job," Bob admitted. "As I recall, most people we talked to were pretty neutral about Barry, though it was clear that he had excellent technical skills. And everything appeared to go well for the first year or so as we chose a vendor for the project. Certainly the reports I was getting from him indicated progress. In fact, I liked the idea that he was setting ambitious goals for his group. It squared with my ideas of accountability. And he seemed to be reaching those milestones."

"I didn't have a chance to thoroughly review those EMR projections you gave me last week," Charlie said, "but my impression was that Barry's reports were on the optimistic side."

"Optimistic verging on misleading," Bob said curtly. "After you came on board, I've had the time to take a closer look at his operations, and he's been dragging his feet. When I question him about what I see as budgetary overruns and staff conflicts, he reacts defensively, as if I've insulted him. He always seems to point his finger at someone else rather than take responsibility. It's impossible to work with someone like that."

"What's happened now?"

"He's starting to avoid me. In fact, he canceled three scheduled meetings with flimsy excuses. He scheduled one of them last week when he knew he would be out of town meeting with the EMR vendor. Now that really pissed me off."

"How did you find out?"

"I decided to drop by his office," Bob said. "He always discouraged me from coming by—and I now see why. The place is a mess. And he left just one staffer to hold the fort—and that fellow didn't seem as if he knew what he was supposed to be doing."

Charlie thought about his visit to the IT department. The impression he got was that the IT department operated as if it had a marginal connection, at best, to the rest of the hospital—and that sort of attitude had to start at the top.

"As it turns out, I had a similar experience last week as well," Charlie said. "I was between meetings, and I decided to stop in. Again, there was just one staff member there. He was friendly enough, although I had the feeling he was not being particularly productive in his job."

The Third Domain of Organizational Excellence

"Maybe Barry's right after all," Bob said. "He blames the staff for the delays in the project. He inherited most of his people when he arrived here, and he told me he thought they were incompetent. So much so, he said, that he had to come up with the IT plan on his own."

"And you took his assessment at face value?" Charlie asked.

"I'm not sure it matters," Bob replied. "The issue is that he's the manager, he's the person responsible for completing the EMR project, and he should be held accountable for not following through on his commitments."

Addressing Bob's Role in the New Dominion

Charlie had to agree that, on the whole, Bob was right about Barry, but there was something about Bob's response and, indeed, his whole handling of the affair, that underscored Bob's own limitations as a leader. The executive team had spent the last month discussing the people side of business, and it was clear, for all his experience and skills, that this was not where Bob's talents lay.

"You've documented your encounters with him?" Charlie asked.

"I have. When he started failing to deliver the numbers he promised, I started taking notes. My comments are contained in his evaluations."

Charlie considered his options. "I agree that he's the wrong person for the job. In fact, I'm not sure that there is a job for him at Dominion," Charlie said. "I think we need to let him go, but before we do, we should check with Sally to make sure that we're covered. From what you've said, I don't think he's going to leave without some sort of protest. I also want you to work with an independent consultant to find out where we are in the EMR process and determine how we can get it back on track as quickly as possible. Is there anything I'm missing?"

"I think that should do it," Bob said, standing up, but he wasn't finished. "I feel as though I should bear some of the responsibility for the situation," Bob went on. "If I hadn't been distracted, I would have figured out what was going on in IT a long time before this."

Charlie smiled. Bob still was a good soldier. He admired Bob for being so scrupulous and, all in all, had to agree that Bob had a hand in Barry's failure. It wasn't just a question of time or attention, though. Bob fell short because he was a poor judge of personality, and he was a poor judge of personality because, when it came down to it, he just didn't think personality was important. All he was interested in were the numbers. Whether Barry was the right person to be producing those numbers was not a real issue for him. Could Bob have been more supportive? Definitely. Could Dominion have found a more suitable post for Barry given his personality? Perhaps. Or did Barry just lack the personality to work in a large organization? It was too late to find out.

"I appreciate your frankness, Bob," Charlie said, meeting Bob's eyes. "I really do, but sit down a second. I have a related issue to talk to you about."

Bob sat down and looked expectantly at Charlie. "You were here before Jim arrived, weren't you?" Charlie asked.

171

The Third Domain of Organizational Excellence

"Actually, I came on just after he was hired," Bob replied.

"But you and he worked out a close and productive working relationship over the years," Charlie continued.

"That's right," Bob said. "I think it fair to say that we had complementary strengths. Jim had a vision for the hospital, and he was naturally charismatic. People liked to follow him. I'm more of a numbers guy. My job was to convert his vision into action and make sure we met our targets."

"My goal is to find a way to re-create that relationship," Charlie said. "I want you in a position where your strengths complement mine. Over the last month or so, I've been encouraging the executive team to explore the people side of business, and although you have some serious reservations about the direction I've been pursuing, you've been willing to hear me out. My impression, though, is that your heart's not in it."

Charlie saw that, despite his efforts to choose his words carefully, the color had drained from Bob's face. "Bob, before I go further, let me reassure you," Charlie said. "You're a key member of the executive team. Your understanding of Dominion and the challenges we face are second to none, but as you've said, you're a numbers guy. My goal is to keep you in a senior role that takes full advantage of your strengths and that works with the more flexible structure I'm trying to create at Dominion.

Bob relaxed slightly, and Charlie went on. "One of the things I'm trying to do is to redefine the nature of leadership at Dominion. In the past, it's been pretty hierarchical, and the bottom line has always been, well, the bottom line. And while holding people accountable for meeting their goals is a critical element in our success, nurturing their leadership skills is equally important. The situation with Barry is just one example of our failure to do this. In retrospect, it's clear that Barry was the wrong person for the job.

"And while Barry didn't make his numbers, I've encountered a number of people at Dominion—Lou Perrott, our head of surgery, comes to mind—who appear to be successful leaders without being particularly effective. Lou regularly meets or exceeds his financial targets, but comes up short in terms of leadership. You heard about one of Lou's surgeons throwing a scalpel during a procedure. That sort of behavior is unacceptable—not simply because it's wrong, but also because it undermines the relationship between the doctors and nurses."

Bob looked abashed. "I think I understand what you're getting at, Charlie. You're trying to take the hospital in a new direction, and I just haven't gotten on board to the extent you might have liked."

Charlie nodded. "There's some truth in that, but nonetheless I'm very grateful that you made your views clear. The executive team thrives on diversity of opinion. When members of the team challenge one another, the result is a solution that's better than something any single one of us can come up with. But I have to find a way that you can be true to yourself and work with me to advance the organization."

"What do you think that will entail?" Bob asked.

The Third Domain of Organizational Excellence

"I've been quite impressed by your ability to think strategically and your grasp of policy and procedure," Charlie said. "I would like to work with you in reshaping your role in ways that really take advantage of your talents. Sound fair?"

"I guess so," said Bob. Charlie noted that Bob looked a little disappointed, although he was trying his best to hide it.

"All I can say, Bob, is that you were in the right role when you worked with Jim. I want you in the right role now that you are working with me. Let's both think about it and get together again in about two weeks."

Now Charlie stood up, and the two men walked toward the door. "Come in with a job description based on your strengths," Charlie said, "and we'll start from there."

The Consulting Team Discusses Developmental Differences

The next day, Charlie arrived at the office having second thoughts about his conversation with Bob, but as the day progressed, his confidence in his decision grew. He needed Bob in a position that took better advantage of Bob's personality and skills and that was a good fit for Dominion, but he hated to have to hurt a committed member of the Dominion family.

On Friday, when Lee and Tom met with him before the executive team meeting, he brought it up. "I don't think anyone at Dominion has ever thought about matching people's temperament and aptitude to their jobs—and now I know why. Not only does it require a fair amount of thought, but you need to be pretty direct about it." Charlie described his conversation with Bob about Barry (which Tom and Lee had been expecting) and then launched into his account of his meeting with Bob (which they hadn't anticipated).

Lee understood Charlie's sympathy for Bob. "That must have been hard for both of you," he said, "but you did the absolutely right thing, both for Bob and for Dominion. Taken as a group, people share all the attributes we've described in the first five principles. They look for safety and security, for instance, and they welcome the opportunity to grow and achieve mastery. How individuals express these attributes depends a great deal on their personalities—the product of their genes, brain structure, and formative experiences. Some individuals are more intellectually gifted, while others are more socially savvy. Some are introverted, while others are extroverted. Bob is not a good judge of people. Nonetheless, as you've said, he has unmatched institutional knowledge, a knack for policy, and a heartfelt commitment to the institution. These qualities are very valuable to Dominion."

Tom picked up the thread. "Different personal styles and skills are needed for different positions in the organization. One size does not fit all, so one of your principle challenges as CEO is to make sure you have the right people in the right jobs on your executive team.

"For instance, the CFO position requires attention to business and an almost intuitive understanding of numbers. Henry fits the role. Other jobs require a high degree of interpersonal sensitivity and emotional intelligence. Sally, in her role as vice president for HR, has these characteristics in abundance. Other jobs require a fair amount of technical expertise. Ryan, as medical director, is a good example of this.

The Third Domain of Organizational Excellence

"But there are two things you have to keep in mind. First, if you ignore personality and treat people as if they were indistinguishable—something that Bob tends to do—you fail to harness the talents of leaders like Julie and allow less competent people, like Debbie, to slip by.

"Second, regardless of their particular strengths, leaders have to have some consciousness of all three domains we talked about earlier—business, technical, and people. And if one of these areas is underdeveloped, you must challenge them to develop some level of fluency if not mastery in it."

"In a way, that's what I'm trying to do with Bob," Charlie said. "He's never going to be a people person, so I think he's eventually going to like being in a role where worrying about the people side of business is not a major part of his responsibilities. At the same time, I'm going to continue to challenge him to develop his ability to factor people into his decisions."

"That's a good way of looking at it," Tom continued. "As we've been saying, people like challenges. They look for opportunities for growth and mastery, and Bob is no exception.

"Of course, we're not the only ones to make the point that the role of a good manager is to find the right jobs for each member of the team. *First, Break All the Rules* also emphasizes the need to find the right roles for people. As its authors see it, one of the keys to managerial success is to 'Help each person find the right fit.'"

"That's right," Charlie said, "but as a manager, I can tell you that hiring the right person in the first place is equally important and equally difficult. It's all too easy to make a mistake that will hold you back for months."

"Here again, considering the people side of business can help," Lee observed. "People tend to be hired for their intellectual abilities. In fact, their emotional capacity to handle the job is just as important. Debbie knows nursing, but her personality leaves her struggling as a leader."

Problematic Employees

"And then there's Barry," Charlie said. "He seemed to have a sound understanding of how the EMR could help the hospital, but as head of IT he pursued his own agenda without regard for the good of the organization or his responsibilities as a team leader."

"So, unlike Bob, you don't buy Barry's assertion that his team was at fault for the delays in the EMR?" asked Tom.

"I see you picked up on that," Charlie replied. "I was a little taken aback that Bob seemed to accept Barry's explanation without questioning it. His reaction just confirmed my feeling that his inability to judge personality was undermining his effectiveness. He wasn't particularly interested in finding out what went wrong in IT. He just wanted to hold Barry accountable for his failure to deliver the numbers."

"We've seen many people like Barry in the course of our careers, those who, for one reason or another, don't function well in an organizational setting," Lee said. "I guess you could call them developmentally impaired.

"These individuals are the most difficult employees to assess and address. They are very good at presenting themselves as high functioning and technically competent. In fact, they often appear especially competent or confident during the hiring process. They mask their own self-doubt and express without reservation an ability to handle the most challenging problems. Early in their tenure they can maintain their façade of superiority, but events usually catch up with them. They typically bite off more than they can chew, and as this becomes apparent, they reveal the deep-seated developmental and emotional problems that caused them to overestimate their abilities in the first place. Their sarcasm, their deflection of blame, their refusal to cooperate are all stratagems they use to try to maintain their inflated image and hide their failings."

"I guess I feel sorry for Barry," Charlie remarked. "But how do you get someone like that to change?"

"You probably can't," Tom said. "We've said it before, but it's worth saying again: it's not your responsibility to get anyone to change. You can create a supportive environment so that people have the opportunity to change and grow—and if it's possible, you can reconfigure their positions so that someone with a specific personality has a better chance of succeeding and serving the organization—but getting people to change is not part of your job description.

"Furthermore, there are some people who are just not going to respond to your efforts, and Barry is likely one of them. People like Barry have selective filters that make it almost impossible to assimilate negative feedback. They respond defensively because any feedback that challenges their inflated self-concept is intolerable. It's common for them to refuse to sign performance-improvement plans, because signing would force them to acknowledge that a problem exists. They often respond to interventions by filing a grievance."

"So what can we do?" Charlie asked.

"It's critical that you use the same approach you would use with any employee: providing support, encouraging professional development, and insisting on accountability. You should apply your organizational rules and structure in a very clear, consistent, and impersonal way. Also, consult with people in Sally's department to make sure you're following correct procedure. You never know how things will turn out, and if the employee fails to change, at least you've gone by the book. That approach is fair to the employees, and it protects you."

"What are the odds that someone like Barry will work out?"

In *Results That Last*, Quint Studer places people like Barry in what he calls the low-performance group—about 8 percent of employees—and prescribes much the same approach for dealing with them that we've been talking about: close monitoring, careful performance reviews, clear expectations, and specific consequences. In his experience, one third will improve to adequate levels while two thirds will need to leave. Half of those who leave will do so on their own."

"How do you distinguish between employees who are just in over their heads from those, like Barry, who are developmentally impaired?"

"Frankly, it's hard to know, at least initially," Lee responded. "When you apply the balance of support and structure that's the essence of our framework, people will begin to sort themselves out. In particular, people who are developmentally impaired do not respond well to structure. They are a bit like compass needles that point south. They move in a direction counter to the goals and culture of the organization. People who want to do well but underperform have an inner compass that points in the right direction, but have trouble getting there. They will generally respond positively to support and structure, and benefit from being moved to a position that's a better fit for their talents."

THE DEVELOPMENTALLY IMPAIRED EMPLOYEE WORKS COUNTER TO EFFORTS OF THE TEAM

"It's pretty clear from what you've described that Barry is one of those developmentally impaired people," Charlie said. "He has responded to any sort of structure—even my request that he simplify the process of vetting patient information for that nurse in pediatrics—as a violation of his integrity. And that's just my experience. He's gone his own way for most of the time he's been here. Although it would have been better if I had intervened earlier, I think the plan I worked out with Bob conforms to most of your suggestions."

"It's often the case with people like Barry that their developmental impairment stems, at least in part, from their childhood experiences with their families," said Lee. "But it's worth noting that difficult family situations don't always produce poor performers. Didn't you mention to me that Sally said her father was an alcoholic? Children of alcoholics often have a variety of personality issues, but they tend to be really good at trying to head off crises before they occur, a talent that organizations can put to good use."

Charlie looked at his watch. "This conversation about Bob and Barry has set my mind at rest. It's been a real help. But we have to get to the executive team meeting. What I might do is see if I can encourage some perspectives from the team about how they view individual differences."

"That sounds like it might be productive," Tom said. "Let's get over there."

The Executive Team Reviews Individual Differences

When the three of them entered the conference room, it was all Charlie could do not to break into a grin. Julie had moved to the other side of the table and was sitting next to Henry, and Sally had positioned herself at the corner of the table next to Ryan. Clearly, working together on the MRSA project had brought them closer.

Charlie asked Bob to open the meeting with a status report on the new clinic, and then Julie went over her goals for the website update. After each presentation, there was a fair amount of debate. Charlie limited himself to making sure the conversations stayed on point. When they had wound down, he mentioned that he wanted to continue the discussion they had been having about the people side of business.

The Third Domain of Organizational Excellence

"We had to cut our conversation on accountability a little short last week," he said. "Does anyone have any additional thoughts they would like to share?"

Ryan leaned forward. "As most of you know, I've had an issue lately with one of my long-term employees. She thought she was entitled to promotion to unit manager by virtue of seniority, but our selection committee found that another candidate was more qualified. I just assumed that because she understood the structure, she would accept the decision. After all, our system of accountability is pretty transparent. Boy, was I wrong! She filed a grievance, claiming age discrimination.

"I'll be frank. I was initially very angry. We had gone to great lengths to create a fair evaluation process—something that as an African American is very important to me—and I felt somehow that she doubted my sincerity. But, after talking to Sally, I realized that I had evaded my responsibility. I had let the system hold her accountable, rather than meeting with her and explaining why she came up short. I just shied away from delivering some hard truths and helping her accept them."

"That's a really good point, Ryan," Charlie said. "When you avoided following up, the balance between structure and support was thrown out of alignment. There's no guarantee how the nurse would have reacted, but if she was a reasonable person she would have benefited from your personal support."

"In fact, that's what happened," Ryan said. "It wasn't an easy conversation, but the result is that she has accepted the decision and seems to be adjusting. I sure feel a lot better."

"But what would have happened if she hadn't been a reasonable person?" Henry asked.

"I've been talking with Tom and Lee about just that point," Charlie replied. "What if she hadn't responded?"

"Charlie used the word *reasonable*," Lee said, "and I think Henry is asking how you define *reasonableness*. I would define a reasonable person as someone who responds well to support and structure and who is able to tolerate disappointment. An unreasonable person is someone who struggles emotionally and who rejects both the support and the structure that managers offer."

"So the nurse in question was a reasonable person by your definition," Henry observed, warming to the topic. "But she could have gone along with the results of the promotion committee without raising a fuss."

"That's true," Tom replied. "But there's no escaping the people side of business. You just have to look around this room to notice that people react differently to a particular situation. There are a number of different parts to this reaction, and sometimes they are difficult to sort out. But as a manager, that's your job.

"One aspect of this is personality, the result of their genes, brain structure, and formative experiences. Aptitude, temperament, character are all ways that we try to describe this essential difference among people. People respond differently to support and structure in a business because of their personalities."

The Third Domain of Organizational Excellence

"That makes managing people a bit more complex, doesn't it?" Bob interjected. Charlie looked at him in surprise. This was a change. Perhaps Bob had never really considered the importance of personal differences, but at least he was doing so now.

"Absolutely," Tom replied. "At the same time, the diversity of perspectives that an organization has at its disposal only makes it stronger. The kind of back-and-forth conversation you were having earlier about the new clinic or the website was a product of the individual perspectives in the room—and I think it resulted in much better decisions."

The Benefits of Cultural Diversity

Listening intently, Julie was compelled to join in. "You are talking about differences in personality. There are other reasons that reasonable people react differently—and from my point of view, the big one is cultural diversity.

"We all talk about diversity at Dominion, but I don't think we fully understand what we're really saying. We're willing to recognize gender, racial, and cultural differences without really dealing with the fact that people with different gender, racial, and cultural experiences approach the world differently. Embracing diversity doesn't just mean accepting people who look different. It means welcoming people who look different and who think differently. As a woman and a Hispanic person, I haven't always felt the perspectives I bring to our deliberations were welcome."

"I have had the same impression from time to time," added Ryan. "Because of my race and because of the culture in which I was raised, the experiences that have shaped my life are very different from those that Sally or Bob might have encountered. Consequently, I haven't shared my insights into some issues because I felt the team might dismiss my viewpoint as being atypical and unacceptable. Sometime I've felt that I should hold myself back, although I'm not particularly proud that I did."

There was an expectant pause—and Charlie spoke up. "As CEO, I have to say that we need diversity, not just because it's fair—though that's part of it—but because it gives us a real competitive advantage. I agree with Tom that the more types of different perspectives each team includes, the stronger and more productive it can be. And that goes for the teams in the operating rooms, in the cafeteria, in the pharmacy, as well as in the executive suite, so if there's something that we're doing that keeps anyone here from speaking freely, I want to know about it, okay?

"Of course, we're going to have to reconcile these perspectives—and once we reach a decision, I expect everyone to get on board," Charlie continued. "We might not always make the right choice, but I want us all to take responsibility for our failures as well as our successes."

Noticing time running short, Charlie closed out the meeting and presented the plan for the coming week. "You received an e-mail about an executive team retreat next Friday. Tom and Lee have learned a lot about Dominion over the last six weeks, and they'll run the workshop. In the morning, they'll be sharing with you their framework for the people side of business, some of which we've already touched on in our meetings. In the afternoon, we'll focus on the leadership implications of this framework. I'm looking forward to digging into these issues as a team."

Reflecting on Diversity, Discrimination, and Performance

When the three of them had settled themselves around the conference table in Charlie's office, Charlie admitted that the diversity discussion had taken him a bit by surprise.

"You wouldn't have known it, Charlie, from the way you responded," Tom said. "You made a really good case for it."

"Thanks to Julie," Charlie replied. "While I've appreciated the importance of diverse ideas intellectually, I don't think I've fully understood its importance from an operational point of view. We're talking about strategic advantage, not political correctness. But I can imagine situations in which people might think they're being discriminated against when they're not."

"There's much good research on just that subject," said Tom. "Members of minority groups sometimes perceive subtle forms of discrimination that just don't register for majority group members. I'll bet, for instance, that none of the white members of the executive team could have pinpointed the reasons why Ryan occasionally holds back, but studies have shown that there usually is something there. Of course, how individuals react to discrimination is a reflection of their individual differences.

"As Ryan himself indicated during the executive team meeting, it works both ways. His experiences with discrimination and the value he placed on fair process blinded him to his

186

responsibility to address the emotional needs of his employees. At the same time, people sometimes claim discrimination when there are other things going on. Joyce claimed age discrimination, but she was reacting in part to her personal situation. Sorting out real from perceived discrimination is always a challenge for leadership."

"But I can envision a situation where you would be hard pressed to decide whether people are being discriminated against," Charlie said. "Let me give you an example. Jim and Bob used to start major meetings with the Lord's Prayer. I dropped the practice because I thought it wrong from the perspective of diversity, but dropping it could appear to some people as discrimination."

"There's no easy answer to your question," Lee said. "There are situations where not everyone is going to be happy, but you need to be willing to at least discuss your position, hear objections, and strive for consistency and fairness."

"That strikes me as the right approach," Charlie replied. "I assume you have to deal with this sort of issue as it comes up."

He paused for a second. "I know it's getting late, but I had a thought about Bob that I wanted to run by you. You heard his presentation about the new clinic. I thought he was very, very good. He does a great job analyzing this sort of thing. I'm thinking of adding strategic development and special projects to his new portfolio. There's certainly no one at Dominion who has a comparable feel for our potential and the market."

"That sounds like a great idea," Lee observed. "And I think it will appeal to Bob. I would also recommend that you extend your notion of finding the best fit to the rest of your executive team. They all would benefit from opportunities for their growth and mastery based on their personal strengths and weaknesses, and so would Dominion."

"Give me an idea of what you have in mind," Charlie replied.

"The events of the last six weeks have shown that you have a group of people who, when provided a balance of support and structure, turn out to be *optimal performers*," said Lee. "I would put Sally, Julie, and Ryan in that category. They've all really bloomed. They have healthy personalities, and they fit their roles perfectly. Your job is to continue to provide challenges so that they continue to improve.

"There is a second category of individuals who are *good performers*. Henry is a good example of this category. While he has good skills for his job, and therefore is a very good fit for his position, he is deficient in his people skills—although even here he is growing. You need to work on this with him. Since he seems to be getting along so well with Julie, you might ask her to collaborate with him as he creates a more effective team atmosphere in the billing department and learns to engage the skills of people like Dan Welch, who has an abundance of experience and a real desire to contribute.

"Debbie is someone we might call a *marginal performer*. It's going to take a close application of support and structure to get her on track. You need to define her areas of deficiency and develop a tailored plan for her growth. For example, Debbie performs marginally because she is not assertive; she's passive and reactive. At the same time, she is committed to the hospital and is extremely knowledgeable about nursing. To maximize her potential, you're going to have to provide her leadership training—perhaps a coach—and you'll need to evaluate her progress periodically.

"Finally, there are those individuals who, no matter what level of support and structure, are *failed performers*. They fail to meet their responsibilities and diminish the effectiveness and productivity of the organization. Barry represents an individual in this category and needs to be a *former performer*."

"I think you've nailed it," Charlie remarked. "I need to think more about what I want to do in each case."

"Great," Tom responded, "you might also give some thought to the leadership implications of each of our six principles. That's going to be the topic of the afternoon session at the retreat next week—and is something that you and your team will need to address in your own unique way."

"I thought I was going to have a week off," Charlie remarked, "but I guess a CEO's work is never done."

The Third Domain of Organizational Excellence

Principle 6: Individuals are different from one another.

1. Individuals are different from one another and work best in positions that reflect these differences. Some individuals, for instance, are more intellectually gifted and others are more socially savvy. Some are more introverted, while others are more extroverted. The various roles of an organization require different personal styles and skills, and managers should try to match employees' talents—emotional as well as intellectual—to their job requirements.

2. Some people have difficulty being contributing members of an organization because their psychological development is impaired or interrupted. They tend to blame others for poor performance and undermine their teams in various ways. These people can be exceedingly difficult to work with. The manager's role is not to change them, but to develop a careful plan for support and structure. In many cases, organizations ultimately have to release these people.

3. An organization needs people with diverse perspectives to maximize its productivity. People may be different because of race, gender, sexual orientation, or ethnic background. Diversity enriches the intellectual, social, and cultural environment of the organization and enhances the organization's ability to define and meet its goals. Diversity is an asset for the organization as long as people are willing to reconcile their diverse perspectives for the good of the organization.

CONCLUSION

LEADERSHIP BASED ON PSYCHOLOGICAL PRINCIPLES

A week later, the executive team assembled at the retreat center at the top of Green Mountain, a 15-mile drive from Dominion. Charlie had assumed that they would meet in the hospital's conference room, but on Monday morning he had received a detailed e-mail from Henry suggesting a number of off-site locations and listing the pros and cons of each. Charlie was a little surprised as he scanned the message, but also pleased. Henry was discovering the satisfaction of contributing as a team player.

Henry was also right to suggest holding the meeting at another location. Moving it out of the hospital was an opportunity for team members to get to know each other better. Charlie had his assistant check out Henry's suggestions, and they decided on Green Mountain. The local parks department maintained the center, whose heavy log beams and stone fireplace revealed its origins as the summer retreat of a wealthy 19th-century textile executive. "The executive lifestyle certainly has changed," Charlie thought wryly, trying to imagine what it would be like being out of range of his smartphone for more than a few hours.

During the morning session, Tom and Lee would formally introduce the six principles to the team. Charlie had been referring to the principles individually at the executive meetings, but now that he understood them as a coherent whole, he wanted to make sure that the team had the same broad understanding.

The afternoon session would focus on the leadership implications of the principles. After all, that was the purpose of the framework that Tom and Lee had developed: creating a context for leaders to think in new ways about their role in the organization. Charlie wanted the members of his team to consider the specific things they would do differently, and one way to do this would be to have them to take responsibility for leading the afternoon session.

As he envisioned it, the six members of the executive team in attendance—Bob, Sally, Henry, Julie, Ryan, and Debbie—would pair up to cover the six principles, each person co-leading the discussion of two principles. Barry had not been invited. To make matters even more interesting, they would make their presentations with different partners. The team members would take an hour to talk through their first presentation before lunch. After lunch, they would switch partners and work on their second presentation for an hour and then spend the rest of the afternoon in discussion. Tom and Lee weren't sure how this was going to work—It wasn't the way they regularly proceeded—but they were game.

After the staff gathered in comfortable armchairs in front of the fireplace, Charlie stood up and surveyed the faces that were so critical to the future of Dominion. He had a sense that he had come to know his team members much better in the last few weeks, their strengths as well as their weaknesses, and it occurred to him that this was the first critical step in mastering the people side of the business.

Charlie kept it simple. "I don't have to tell any of you that these are unforgiving times. Funding is tight, and the competition is intense. We all have to perform at the very top of our game if Dominion is to flourish.

"One of the things that really resonated with me when I first met Tom and Lee was their insistence that an organization had to do well in all three domains to be successful: the technical domain, the business domain, and the people domain. I couldn't agree more. Dominion has always been good at the first two. We are widely respected for the quality of the medical care we provide and admired for the skill with which we manage our operations. We're good in these areas because we've worked at it. But Dominion has never paid much attention to the people side of business, and that has taken a toll on our bottom line.

"In the past we could afford to be inattentive, but not any longer. The people side of business integrally relates to the technical and business domains. When we ignore the people side of business, we jeopardize everything that we have worked so hard to accomplish.

"We all know the facts. A people problem—our failure to follow standard infection control procedures—was at the heart of the MRSA outbreak. Another people problem—our inability to foster respect between doctors and nurses—led to operating room protocol being violated in ways that could have had serious repercussions for our staff, our patients, and this institution.

The Third Domain of Organizational Excellence

"Similarly, on the business side of our organization, a people problem—our failure to provide opportunities for growth and mastery—led directly to unacceptably high turnover among our nurses. Another people problem—our inability to create a caring environment at Dominion—has caused patient dissatisfaction. By and large, patients have no reservations about the quality of care we deliver. They are disappointed with the way we deliver this care.

"So the six principles that Tom and Lee developed are not in the category of 'nice to know.' When we understand them, when we internalize them, they become our margin of excellence."

Presenting the Six Principles

Tom and Lee took the end of Charlie's talk as their cue. Tom stood up, "As you know, we've been working with Charlie to get to know Dominion over the last six weeks. At the same time, we've been taking Charlie step by step through the six core psychological principles that managers should know to lead their people effectively. You've been discussing some of these ideas at your Friday meetings. Now it's time to put all the pieces together."

Then Lee took over. "Some of what we have to say will be familiar to you. You might remember it from your college psychology classes. Other concepts will be new, and we're happy to introduce them to you. Thanks to advances in research, we now know more than ever before about how the brain is wired and how we, as human beings, interact with the world. These fresh insights are fundamental to our six principles.

"Another place where you may have encountered some of these ideas is in the management books on your shelf. Each author approaches management from his or her own perspective, and while some touch on psychology, none provides a comprehensive overview of the basic psychological needs that shape the way people act on the job. Once you understand these six psychological principles, you'll return to classics like *The 7 Habits of Highly Successful People*, *First, Break All the Rules*, and *Good to Great* with new eyes."

Tom added, "But our point is not just to make you better readers. It's to give you a framework that you can return to again and again to meet the challenges of leadership. It's a way of looking at your organization and reexamining your role. What do you do about an uncooperative employee who sabotages team performance? How do you balance support with the need to hold your staff accountable? How can you accommodate individual autonomy and teamwork? Anything that has to do with the way people act at work falls under our framework.

"But here's the flip side. Leaders who don't understand or even recognize the psychological responses that people bring to work, who fail to incorporate these fundamental psychological insights in their approach to management, will never be able to harness these responses to meet their organization's goals. They are always going to underperform. Smart leaders will use these basic facts of life as a starting point, adjust their leadership strategy appropriately, and create a more productive, more motivated workforce."

Lee stepped to the flip chart and wrote the numbers one to six down the left side. "Let's begin at the beginning," he said. "The first principle grounds us in the latest thinking about evolutionary psychology. It states that human responses reflect the underlying design of the brain, which has evolved over hundreds of thousands of years for survival. Primitive emotions like the need for security take precedence over higher-order rational processes."

"And that means that if you expect people to act in purely rational ways, you're kidding yourself," added Tom. "People are people are people, not Vulcans."

"The next three principles explore the nature of the human need for support and growth, two drives that evolution has hard-wired into us to ensure our survival," Lee continued, drawing an arc connecting numbers 2, 3, and 4. "Principle 2 underscores the human need for safety and security and the strategies people take to achieve that safety. From a leadership point of view, this means that it is up to you to make sure your people feel cared for in ways that are meaningful to them.

"The third principle is that people working together can't help but look at their situation in terms of family structures and dynamics. It's pretty straightforward. People are programmed to find security in family. It's a template they use not only when they are young but throughout their lives."

Tom picked up the thread. "Principle 4 explains that healthy people want to master their world, and so look for opportunities for growth. The roots of this phenomena, like Principles 2 and 3, lie in our evolutionary past. Our ancestors flourished in prehistoric times not simply because they had reasoning skills but also because they liked using them. It's no surprise that research consistently identifies the attainment of mastery as the most important source of job satisfaction. People want to grow in their jobs and take on new challenges, and they value the guidance a leader can provide in helping them achieve new levels of mastery.

"But people don't just need support to flourish in a social environment. They need structure as well. This gets us to our fifth principle. We contend that the need for structure is as hard-wired into human circuitry as the need for support. People feel most comfortable when they operate within a well-defined framework."

Tom pulled out a diagram showing the balance of support and structure, based on acceptance of human design in the context of individual differences.

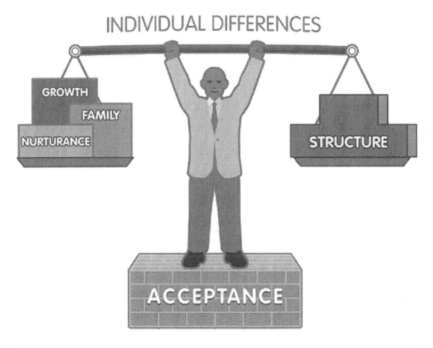

THE BALANCE OF SUPPORT AND STRUCTURE, BASED ON ACCEPTANCE, IN THE CONTEXT OF INDIVIDUAL DIFFERENCES

Lee added, "We understand how strongly many of you feel about holding people accountable, and we agree that's important. Our purpose is to position accountability not as an end in itself but as a complementary tool for leading people, one that reflects a basic human need."

In the first principle, the focus is on the evolutionary heritage that we all share as human beings. In the sixth, it's on the variations in human responses caused by our inherited genetic code and our unique formative experiences, gender, culture, and race. These individual differences account for variability in the way staff members respond to the universal needs described in the Principles 2 through 5. Harness these differences, and you harness a great source of strength and energy for your organization."

Tom looked around at the members of the executive team, who up to this point had been sitting intently in their armchairs. "Any questions?"

There was a pause, and then Julie said. "So this is what you and Charlie have been up to. Intuitively, the framework makes sense. I suppose the next step is to go over it from the top in more detail."

"That's exactly our plan," said Tom.

Two hours later the discussion wound down, and Charlie again stood up and looked at his team members. He had been watching them closely during the discussion, limiting his participation to helping Tom and Lee stay on schedule. It was important, he thought, for his executives to think through the principles on their own. In the meantime, he had come to some conclusions about how he wanted to divide the group for their presentations. He decided to mix it up. He wanted to draw on the strengths of his team members, but also put them in situations where they could learn from their partners.

"It's eleven," he said. "Let's take an hour before lunch and an hour after lunch to work on your presentations on the leadership implications of the six principles. This is how I'd like to divide the group.

"For the morning prep session, I'd like Ryan and Debbie to focus on the leadership implications of Principle 1: *The design of the brain determines human behavior.* They're our medical experts, and they're most familiar with the biology behind the principle.

"Bob and Sally get Principle 2: *People are most productive in an emotionally safe and supportive atmosphere.* Sorry, Bob. I couldn't help myself.

"Henry and Julie will focus on Principle 3: *People working together tend to replicate family structures and dynamics.*"

"With my family, we could end up running long," Julie remarked. Henry looked baffled but curious.

"For the afternoon prep session," Charlie continued, "I'd like Sally and Debbie to take a look at Principle 4: *People want an opportunity for growth to acheive mastery.* I know that personal development is something both of you care deeply about.

199

The Third Domain of Organizational Excellence

"Bob and Julie are to take Principle 5: *People need structure to shape and motivate their behavior.* That should make up, Bob, for having to work on support.

"And finally, Ryan and Henry will present the leadership implications of Principle 6: *Individuals are different from one another.* Enjoy!

"One last thing," he added. "I want you to come up with a two- or three-word declarative sentence describing the leadership implications of each principle. It should start with the word *leaders*.

"Can you give us an example?" said Henry.

"Sure," said Charlie. "*Leaders always answer questions.* I can't wait to see what you come up with."

The Executive Team Explores the Leadership Implications of the Six Principles

At two o'clock, Charlie announced that it was time to start the discussion of how the six principles affected leadership and that each team would have a half hour. Charlie added that the purpose of the session was to get them to start thinking in terms of the people side of leadership. "The six principles that Tom and Lee formulated are the foundation for a new mindset," he said. "The value of that mindset—and the way you embody it as leaders—will become progressively clearer the more you use it.

"There is a lot riding on the leadership you provide. As members of the executive team, you set the tone for the entire organization. People naturally take their lead from you, they see Dominion through your actions, and they depend on you for both support and structure. If you make these principles your own, then the organization will as well."

Charlie cleared his throat. "I'm ready at the flip charts. Without further ado, let's have Debbie and Ryan start the discussion of the first principle: *The design of the brain determines human behavior.* Would you begin by revealing your tagline for the principle?"

"Sure," Debbie replied. "It's 'Leaders accept people.'"

"Wow," Sally said, "That's not what I would have come up with."

"Me neither," Henry added. "I might have used that to describe the second principle, about the need to be supportive."

"Let me explain," Debbie said.

<u>Leaders Accept People</u>

"One way to look at the first principle is that people are people," she said. "They are not thinking machines. They don't possess superpowers. They are inherently messy. What's more, the first principle tells me that this messiness is somewhat predictable."

"That's right," Ryan added. "The structure of the brain and the way our brains function—and consequently the way we react in the world—reflect our evolution. The actions of our primitive brains are so deep-seated, so much part of who we are, that we take them for granted and don't even think about them. And they are all the more easy to ignore or downplay because our culture places such a premium on acting rationally. But if you're in a leadership position and you make the assumption that people are rational actors, you're going to be baffled. One of the major implications of Principle 1 is that leaders need to accept the mix of nonrational and rational in their employees."

"When we say, 'Leaders accept people,'" Debbie added, "what we mean is that leaders accept people the way they are constructed biologically."

"I agree wholeheartedly," Julie said. "But I've been listening to the way you've been talking about rationality and nonrationality, and I think our tendency to value rational thought over nonrational thought is still coloring the discussion. Maybe it's the marketer in me that's being oversensitive, but I think we're assuming that nonrational thought is what makes people messy. Maybe there's another, less judgmental word besides *messy* that we can use.

"How about *complicated?*" Bob suggested. "That's really the point, correct?"

"Bob's right," Sally said. "As leaders we need to accept human complexity—and that means accepting that humans have emotions."

"I hate to say it, guys, but those of us in marketing have long ago accepted the fact that people have emotions," Julie added. "We appeal to people's emotions all the time. We try to make that emotional connection because we know that emotions preempt logic. What Tom and Lee are giving us is the biological explanation for that fact."

"So, are we saying that leaders need to relate to people on an emotional level?" asked Henry skeptically. "Exactly what does that mean? I wouldn't know how to do it."

"I think you're selling yourself short, Henry," Charlie interjected. He had been meaning to stay on the sidelines of the discussion, but he couldn't help himself. "Let me give you an example. I know you and your team work very hard each year pulling together the financials for our annual report. And I happen to know that you have been known to throw a little party for your group when you hand it in."

"Well, it's a little party," Henry said.

"But you know what I mean. Everyone feels a sense of accomplishment, and you recognize it with a little celebration. If that's not relating to people on an emotional level, nothing is. You don't have to do it."

"Charlie's example is a good one," Ryan added. "We tend to think of emotions as a negative thing, something to work around. In this case, Henry used the emotions he and his team shared—the passion for doing the job and the sense of satisfaction in doing it well—to pull them together."

"I guess I did," Henry said sheepishly. "I had no idea."

"And that's our point," Lee said, unable to contain himself. "Whether we think of ourselves as people persons or not, we are all people persons by virtue of being human, so it makes sense to start acknowledging it. The people in this room aren't starting from scratch when it comes to addressing the people side of business. We're trying to give you a framework for thinking coherently about it—to recognize what you already do and build on it."

There was a slight pause and then Charlie added, "I would even go a step further. As leaders, I would recommend that we go beyond responding to the passion of others and express our own passion for the job."

"I'm not sure I know what I feel about that," Debbie said. "Too much emotion may not be such a good thing."

"I would say it depends," Sally replied. "Negative emotions—anger, resentment, fear—can be counterproductive. The leader's job is to promote positive emotions that serve the organization, and one way of doing that is to set an example. Another way is to find opportunities to acknowledge and address the negative emotions that interfere with productivity."

"And engaging and transforming negative emotions is one of the leadership implications, at least for me, of Principles 2, 3, and 4," said Ryan. "And I guess structure, in Principle 5, can help as well."

"What do you mean by that?" Bob asked.

"Well, knowing that there is a fair, impersonal structure in place for measuring job performance can go a long way toward reducing negative emotions," Ryan replied.

"I want to step in for a second and make a point about what's happening here," Tom said. "We've divided the framework into six principles, but as you've seen, they all work together. That's because they are all ways of thinking about human psychology and, as Bob has said, it's complicated."

Charlie stood up. "Sorry to cut this discussion short, but it's time to move on to the second principle." He looked at the flip chart. "Here are the implications for leadership that I heard in our discussion that are based on Principle 1: *The design of the brain determines human behavior.*

- Accept people with their rational and nonrational features

- Engage with people on an emotional level

- Recognize that emotion preempts logic

- Speak with passion about the job and the organization.

"That's great," Charlie said. "Let's be clear, though. If we had more time, this list would be longer. We're just catching some of the leadership implications of the principles that occur to us today in the context of this discussion. If we were to meet next year and go through the same exercise—not a bad idea, actually—we would come up with a related, but different, list. I guarantee it."

Charlie turned toward the armchairs where Bob and Sally were sitting. "Ready with Principle 2: *People are most productive in an emotionally safe and supportive atmosphere?*"

"We are indeed," Bob said. "And although it pains me to say so, our tagline is 'Leaders nurture staff.'"

The Third Domain of Organizational Excellence

There was a round of applause and some good-natured kidding.

"As you know, this is not my strong suit," Bob replied, "so I'll defer to Sally to start the discussion."

<u>Leaders Nurture Staff</u>

"From my perspective, Principle 2 means that people perceive that someone at work cares for them," Sally began.

"Wait, wait," Henry broke in. "Define what you mean by *care?* These are professional relationships we're talking about."

Bob looked at Henry sympathetically. "I know where you're coming from, Henry," he said. "In fact, this is exactly the objection I raised with Sally before lunch. But she made a very good argument for caring. First, people come to work looking for security. They come here looking for someone to care. They are happier and more productive if they feel someone cares, and given these circumstances, we would be foolish to withhold caring."

"But that's not what I mean," Henry replied. "How does a leader express caring?"

"It's not as complicated as you might think," Bob replied. "You make sure the people on your team know that they matter. You listen to them when they have something to say and you follow up. You stand up for them when the chips are down. You look for opportunities to praise and encourage them. You make sure they have the resources to do their job. And the great thing about this, except for the last item, is that these measures cost nothing to enact."

"And," Sally said, nodding at Bob, "you spend time with them clarifying their role and setting expectations."

"Hold on a second," Bob said. "As you might expect, I paid particular attention this morning to Principle 5. Isn't clarifying roles and expected outcomes about structure and not support?"

"But isn't this another case where the principles overlap?" Julie asked. "When you clarify a person's role, and you support their success, they are likely to perceive your investment of time as helpful and caring. And it has to feel reassuring for employees when their boundaries are well established and most of the decisions they make about their roles are clear-cut."

"So the message here," Sally said, "is that providing security comes in various guises. Another way a leader provides security is by making sure the team has a welcoming work environment. That's something that Julie does very well and that we all should emulate." Julie broke into a broad grin.

"You also want to make sure that the environment is safe," Sally added. "That's part of being a leader. Obviously, there are liability reasons for ensuring workplace safety, but the bottom line is that as a leader your job is to protect your team."

"Here's something we should think about as part of this principle," Debbie said, "and that's negative feedback. People have a tendency to take things personally—I know I do—and I think a good leader makes sure that any criticism about performance is focused on the performance and not the individual."

"That's a great point," said Ryan. "It's one that I know I need to think more about. It's not just being fair in a performance evaluation, but taking the extra step and letting the person you're evaluating know that you're not rejecting them as a person."

"We've been looking at the situation from the point of view of the people who work for us," Julie added. "They need to feel secure to be really productive and creative on the job—That's the way we're all hard-wired—so as leaders it only makes sense to try to meet that need.

"But what do we, as leaders, get out of the arrangement?" Julie asked, looking at the others. "It's not all one way, and it's something more basic, more fundamental, than performance. It's trust. When we provide the security our employees need, they trust us to lead them. That trust makes our job so much easier. I'd say that's a fair trade."

"That's a great point," Charlie said, "and a good place to end the discussion, since we have to move on. I'm sure I missed a few things, but here's what I wrote down.

"The leadership implications of Principle 2: *People are most productive in an emotionally safe and supportive atmosphere*:

- Actively care for your people

- Provide support and encouragement

- Ensure safety and security

- Connect with your people and avoid rejection"

"That sounds about right," Bob said, and the rest of the group seemed satisfied.

"All right," Charlie continued. "Henry and Julie are next up to discuss the third principle: *People working together tend to replicate family structures and dynamics.* And what's your tagline?"

"As I explained to Henry, I grew up in a strong family," said Julie, "so this one feels natural to me. We propose 'Leaders create work families.' What do you think?"

Leaders Create Work Families

There was a pause as each member of the team scrutinized the tagline. "It's not haiku or anything, but it sounds to me that you and Henry have been very careful about the way you've worded that tagline," Ryan observed. "What do you mean by *work families?*"

"You're absolutely right," Henry replied professorially. "We were careful. People come to work primed to view their experience on the job through the perspective of family relationships. They look at us and see their parents. You can ignore that basic human response or you can find ways to make use of it for the good of the organization—try a little organizational ju-jitsu, if I do say so myself.

"To get back to Ryan's question, the fact is that while we can create a family-like atmosphere in our teams, we are not parents and teams are not, in fact, families. We used the phrase *work families* to make that distinction. A real family supports you as long as possible, even when you don't perform. At work, you'll eventually find yourself looking for a new family if your performance is below par."

"Nonetheless, creating that family-like atmosphere is critical," Julie said. "In this sense, Principle 3 is a logical extension of Principle 2. Most people have a strong drive for security, and when it comes to security, being part of a family is as good as it gets."

"This is interesting," said Debbie. "I've haven't really thought of myself as creating a work family. I've been meeting with the nurses on my team individually. Are there other benefits from creating that family-like atmosphere?"

"From my experience in building teams in marketing, people feel more connected to each other," Julie replied. "And as people become more and more committed to their work family, they begin to share a common sense of purpose, which is a very powerful driver of performance.

"I've also noticed, too, that people feel free to act more independently when the team is functioning as a family. It's not like they go off on their own or anything; they are just more willing to step up on their own initiative and help achieve our team goals."

"That sounds pretty amazing," Debbie replied. "But how do you create that sort of family, especially when it's your job to ensure that everyone is performing at the highest level?"

"There are lots of things you can do," Sally said. "You have to make it a point to treat everyone fairly, honestly, and with respect. This gets back to what Henry was saying about a leader's role as a parent. You set the tone for the family. This should help minimize sibling rivalry.

"You also set the expectations. Good leaders, like good parents, are people who encourage the growth of their team members. Good leaders want team members to mature and eventually replace them as leaders."

"But what does a leader do when people bring their personal experiences to the work family?" Ryan asked. "When that nurse on my team didn't get promoted, she did everything but say straight out it was my fault. If she were a teenager, I would say that she was acting out."

"But the fact is that, although she thought of you on some level as her parent and blamed you for holding her back, you're not her parent," said Sally, "and that's an advantage for you. Although it may be small comfort, she was not really acting out against you as a person; she was acting out against an image that she projected on you. As I understand it, the evaluation process was totally fair. Your only shortcoming was that you didn't provide her with some personal support after the decision was made."

"Which, as a good parent, I would naturally have done," Ryan said. "That's the lesson for me."

"One of the things that we've been talking about here is the one-on-one relationship between parent and child that's replicated in the work family," Henry said. "But the whole point of family is that it's a group. One of the things I realized from my preparation with Julie is that I didn't make any allowances for bringing people together when I renovated the billing department. I thought I was doing something nice for them individually by upgrading their equipment and purchasing new furniture, but while they appreciated the gesture, what they probably really wanted from me was to be brought closer together as a team."

Bob had kept quiet during most of this discussion, but now he took the floor. "That's one of the good things about this retreat," he said. "My sense of what the executive team is all about has changed over the last few months. We all used to come to our Friday meetings to represent the interests of our departments, but now we're starting to act as a real team charged with leading Dominion. I'm not honestly sure I'm completely comfortable with this change, but I can see how it will help Dominion in the long run."

Charlie looked thoughtfully at Bob. "I appreciate what you're saying Bob. I'm hopeful that we will become a strong team and that each of you will build strong teams of your own. Teams are the basic unit of the work family. One of the special functions of the executive team is to bring all the individual teams in the organization into alignment."

Charlie sensed he was becoming a little didactic and stopped himself. "But I could go on," he said, grinning, as he returned to the side of the flip chart.

"Here's what I have. The leadership implications of Principle 3: *People working together tend to replicate family structures and dynamics*:

- Create a family-like atmosphere in the workplace

- Treat all team members fairly, respectfully, and honestly

- Encourage trust and engagement

- Build and support teams"

"Wait a second," Henry said. "I didn't hear anyone saying anything about trust."

"I thought that's what you were getting at when you said that leaders treat all team members fairly," Charlie replied. "Besides, I like having at least four points for each principle.

"Now, on to Principle 4: *People want an opportunity for growth to achieve mastery.* Who's leading that discussion?"

Sally and Debbie stood up. "Our approach to Principle 4 is pretty straightforward," Debbie said. "It's 'Leaders encourage growth.'"

"Can't argue with that," Charlie said. "Tell us more."

<u>Leaders Encourage Growth</u>

"As I understand it, Principle 4 is another support-and-security principle," Debbie said. "Being part of a family is an important source of security for people, as we learned from Principle 3. Another important source is feeling that you're the master of your environment. That's the incentive for learning. People want to grow. I know that, as a nurse, I'm always on the lookout for even the smallest bit of information that can help me take better care of my patients and their families, and most nurses feel the same way. When we cut back on training at Dominion, some of our best nurses left for medical centers with active training programs. As a leader, I want my nurses to have all the development possible."

"In an ideal world, that would be great," said Henry. "But how are we going to pay for all that training?"

"Of course, you're right," Debbie said. "Let me modify that last statement. I want my nurses to have development opportunities that enable them to support the mission and strategic goals of the hospital. How's that?"

"That's better," Henry said, "but I still think it's an expensive goal for a leader, and it's my responsibility to watch out for our bottom line."

"But I don't think you're looking at the big picture," Sally said. "How much does it cost to hire and train a new nurse? How does having new people on board affect the patient experience? How much does it cost us to be wedded to old-fashioned ways of doing nursing? You need to put a number on costs like these to get a better sense of whether training really pays off."

"And there are other, less tangible advantages for us as leaders," Ryan added. "Offering opportunities for professional development is one way we can show we care for our staff. Debbie is right. Principle 4 is in many ways an extension of Principle 2. And it's a powerful way of building teams, which gets us back to Principle 3."

"But let's be honest here," Sally said. "Learning is also risky. Sometimes people are afraid to learn new things because they are afraid they will fail. As leaders, we have to find ways to encourage our employees to take risks, and we should set an example by making lifelong learning part of what we expect of ourselves, and this doesn't always mean executive education. It can mean learning from our staff. One of the things that has started to turn around the atmosphere at Dominion these last few weeks is that everyone knows that Charlie has been spending a fair amount of his time asking questions and listening to staff." Charlie looked pleased as heads turned toward him.

"Let me share with you a technique I use to encourage growth in my marketing staff," Julie said. "As part of their annual evaluations, I ask my staff about their development goals for the coming year, and I encourage them to think about their training in terms of their career goals, 5, 10, and even 20 years into the future. I believe I owe it to them as their leader to help them make sure that in 20 years they have 20 years of experience, not one year of the same experience repeated 20 times over."

"I spoke to someone in billing who had been in the department five or six years," Charlie said, "and I asked him whether he could do it for another five or six years, and he said no. The problem was that he saw no opportunity for growth on the job. No one was particularly interested in supporting his efforts to grow or to take advantage of what he did know about how to improve the billing system."

Debbie got back into the discussion. "That ties in with what Sally was saying about learning from your staff. As part of Sally and Ryan's plan to contain the MRSA outbreak, I reviewed procedures with scores of nurses at the hospital, and there were plenty of teachable moments, opportunities for me to make a small suggestion that could affect the quality of care. I also found inspiration for these teachable moments from the initiative of nurses who had gone out on their own, researched the literature, and found new and better ways of containing the bacteria. I wanted other people to pick up on the knowledge they brought to the organization, while highlighting their willingness to invest their own curiosity."

"Debbie makes a really good point about growth," Lee added. "People who grow bring knowledge back into the organization, which is then able to perform that much better."

"There's another related area I'd like to mention, which picks up on something I said at a Friday meeting a few weeks ago," Sally said. "People need time and energy to grow, so as leaders we need to ensure that people maintain a work-life balance. And that means protecting people from assignments that involve them working long hours for weeks on end."

"I know that I objected to this point when you first mentioned it," Bob said, "but it makes sense to me when you put it that way. I like the idea of people bringing knowledge back to the organization, and I know how exciting and interesting it is to take on a new project and try to master it. In the process of identifying a location for our new clinic, I've learned a lot about how the real estate market works, and I've found it fascinating."

"And I could tell that you were enjoying it," Charlie said. "It's going to help us make a good decision. Our time is just about up, so let me read you what I have.

"The leadership implications of Principle 4: *People want growth opportunities that help them acheive mastery*:

- Encourage professional growth

- Set an example by taking advantage of growth opportunities yourself

- Encourage risk taking

- Ensure employees maintain an effective work-life balance

"Does anyone have anything to add?" Charlie asked. When nobody said anything, he looked around the room. People looked a little tired.

"Speaking of the work-life balance, we're two thirds of the way through the principles. Let's take 15 minutes to recharge our batteries, get some fresh air, and enjoy the view. When we get back, Bob and Julie will give us their take on Principle 5: *People need structure to shape and motivate their behavior.* Before we break, would you mind telling us your tagline?"

"Bob wanted to make sure our point is absolutely clear," Julie said. "It's 'Leaders build structure.'"

"It can't be clearer than that," Charlie said.

Leaders Build Structure

The team reassembled in their armchairs in front of the fireplace 15 minutes later. Julie and Sally had walked over to the lookout next to the lodge, where they could pick out Dominion's towers rising above the city below. In a corner of the room, Bob and Henry had engaged in an animated discussion with Ryan and Debbie; it had sounded like they were talking about the new clinic. Charlie took the time to check in with Tom and Lee. "How do you think things are going?" Charlie asked.

"I'm pretty happy with the discussion," Lee replied. "What do you think?"

"It's going well," Charlie said. "I just wish we had more time. People are raising a lot of interesting points."

"I agree," Tom replied. "But you'll have plenty of time to generate more ideas about the leadership implications of the six principles. The ones that have come out today, although very important, are really just a start. For me, the real significance of what I heard so far is how well this team is functioning. It's a far cry from your description of the meeting you called to deal with the MRSA outbreak."

"That's right," Charlie said. "I had a hard time getting them to even agree on a time to meet. I get the feeling that they are listening to each other more closely now, and that the discussion has a sense of direction. People are building on what the other people are saying, rather than using their remarks as an opportunity to tear them down."

"There's one reason for the change," Lee observed. When Charlie seemed puzzled he added, "Your leadership."

Charlie looked embarrassed, but smiled anyway. "Thanks," he said. "I appreciate that. Well, it's time to move on."

He stood up and said, "We're ready to go, folks. Who's going to introduce the discussion of Principle 5?"

"That would be Bob," Julie said, smiling.

"This is simple," Bob began. "Leaders need to make sure there are clear rules and performance standards for all staff members and the business. Leaders need to hold everyone accountable to the mission of the organization. For me, this is the foundation of leadership. All the support in the world, without accountability, will not ensure the success of the organization. We must make sure we promote employees who are strong performers and rid ourselves of staff members who are poor performers. However, I've come to realize is that it's not an either/or proposition. You have to have support *and* accountability."

"I agree with Bob," said Julie. "Accountability and support are both essential for our success. The difficult task for leaders is doing both. Some leaders lean toward accountability and find supporting people difficult. Others who lean toward the support side find that holding people accountable when they fall short on their performance is similarly difficult."

"I'm definitely in the last group," said Debbie, "so I could use some insight here. How do you hold someone accountable in ways that show you care?"

"I would imagine that clear statements about the gap between expectations and actual performance are essential," Ryan said. "If we sound judgmental or punitive—if we make it personal—then we're off track. We have to offer constructive feedback."

The Third Domain of Organizational Excellence

"I agree," Sally said. "In my experience, people with a reasonable outlook tolerate negative feedback reasonably well as long as it is not perceived as a personal attack. Of course, it helps to have solid relationships with your employees in the first place. This goes back to the idea of trust that Charlie maintains we've been talking about. If you have a good relationship with them, employees will understand that you are not rejecting them as people, but commenting on their performance. If you have established this trust and are clear about the changes you would like to see, employees are more willing and better able to make the changes you need."

Henry had been listening to Sally attentively. "I completely agree with you about the need to balance support and accountability, but my problem is the opposite of Debbie's. I'm just not a demonstrative kind of guy. I know I can hold staff accountable to our goals and outcomes, but can we crusty old guys do that other stuff?"

"There are many styles of good leadership, Henry," Tom said, stepping into the discussion. "And that includes the crusty style. From what we've seen, you obviously care about the hospital and the people who work here, and, as you've admitted, you occasionally throw parties for your people to celebrate an accomplishment. You need to let people know that you care. People read leaders carefully to understand their motivation, their concern, and their commitment to people, not just their technical knowledge of the business. The leader's attitude matters, and you can't fake it. If you genuinely balance support and structure, people will perceive it. So, crusty leaders can also be caring leaders."

"I guess I can settle for that," Henry replied.

"We've been talking so far about what we need to do as leaders in our individual relationships with our employees," Julie said. "But we are not just responsible for holding people accountable; we have an obligation to create that structure. I think it's the responsibility of the executive team to develop a clear vision of where we want Dominion to go. In practical terms, we must define the goals and outcomes for success at Dominion."

"That's a good idea," Ryan said. "I've been thinking we should create a strategic plan so everybody at Dominion knows where we're heading as an organization. I've always been a bit taken aback that we've never had one."

"You're right," Charlie said. "I've been thinking the same thing, but I've held off until we began to gel as a group. That's something we should be putting on our agenda. In the meantime, let's see how we've done with Principle 5. Here are some of the ideas you've mentioned:

"The leadership implications of Principle 5: *People need structure to shape and motivate their behavior.*

- Make sure there are clear rules and performance standards

- Hold everyone accountable

- Assess performance, not people

- Provide constructive feedback on performance

The Third Domain of Organizational Excellence

"Does anyone have anything to add?" Charlie said, looking around.

"Okay, on to our last principle. Ryan and Henry will present the leadership implications of Principle 6: *Individuals are different from one another.* Do you want to reveal your tagline?

"Sure," Ryan said. "It's 'Leaders embrace healthy diversity.' As Tom said this morning, the sixth principle is the counterpart of the first. The first principle focuses on processes we all share as human beings. The sixth explores the variations in human responses to the need for support and structure."

<u>Leaders Embrace Healthy Diversity</u>

Ryan stood up. "I have a confession to make. As an African American physician, one of the things that's always irked me about the profession is the way many of my colleagues treat people as if they were completely interchangeable and inferior. That's part of what happened in the operating room when Dr. Bartholomew threw his scalpel. We have to have defined roles, but it's all too easy for us to see people as their roles, rather than appreciate them as individuals and value them for their unique qualities. That's my starting point. What's your approach, Henry?"

"I too have a confession," Henry replied. "I have to admit that I'm one of those people who didn't pay much attention to individual differences, but you know I hate waste, and I'm beginning to see how wasteful this approach is. To truly support people, we must first get to know them as individuals. Because if we don't, we don't fully tap the talent we have and even set some people up for failure, which is as costly to us as it is painful for them."

"In my job in HR I am constantly reminded that there are individual differences between people," Sally said. "As leaders we must recognize that different people are needed in different jobs. There's interesting research that says we tend to hire people like ourselves. It is challenging to hire a person who is truly the best fit for the job. I give Jim great credit for hiring some different faces into roles here at Dominion. That took awareness and nerve."

"Of course I too appreciate Jim's willingness to bring in new faces," Ryan said with some emphasis, "but we should take it a step further. We should do more than accept diversity; we should embrace it. Personally, I think this is the right thing to do."

Ryan looked around at the other executives. He went on, "And when you consider embracing diversity through the lens of the people side of business, it is the professional thing to do. Acknowledging individual differences is the first step in providing the support we know is so important. We also need different ideas, perspectives, and skill sets to achieve success, which is often the result of bringing together people with different backgrounds—women, minorities, and people with different sexual orientations—as well as different personalities."

"The challenge for leaders, then, is harnessing these individual differences," Sally observed. "When it comes to managing people in their jobs, we often try to jam a round peg into a square hole. When that doesn't work out, our solution is to replace the round peg with a square peg. We should at least spend some time deciding whether we can work with a round peg. In other words, we should try to adjust people's job descriptions so that their jobs better fit who they are. I think the results would surprise us."

"But what happens when you run into people who are incapable of functioning productively, who undermine the organization no matter how you try to accommodate them?" Bob asked. "What do you do in this kind of situation?" He was clearly thinking of Barry, whose presence at the meeting wasn't missed.

"From an HR perspective, inadequate and failing performers need the greatest application of support and accountability," said Sally. "You really need to stay focused on them, providing frequent, consistent, and specific feedback on their performance. You may even suggest they get counseling. And if they don't begin to move with the organization, it's your responsibility as a leader to let them go."

"Let me just underline that point," said Lee. "It's not your responsibility to change a poorly performing employee. It's their responsibility."

"That's a relief!" said Bob.

"Anyone else?" asked Charlie. When there was no response, he said, "Here we go. The leadership implications of Principle 6: *Individuals are different from one another.*

- Appreciate your employees as individuals

- Adjust job descriptions to fit their strengths

- Embrace healthy diversity in all its aspects

- Deal firmly and fairly with counterproductive individuals

"Is that a fair description?" There was a general nodding of heads. "Okay, I'll have these flip charts typed up and sent out to you all on Monday."

Wrapping Up the Workshop

"Okay, folks," Charlie said. "This has been a very productive day, and it's certainly given us all things to think about. I'd like for all of you to consider what we've discussed today, reflect on your strengths and weaknesses as leaders, and send me a memo with a set of three goals for personal leadership development with some suggestions about training that might be useful. You can use Sally as a resource for this. Think of it as an application of Principle 4. In the meantime, have a good weekend; I look forward to seeing you all on Monday."

After the executive team headed out to their cars, Tom and Lee joined Charlie at the overlook. "I was pleased the way the workshop went," Charlie said. "I think we are going to see some dramatic changes in the quality of our leadership in the next few months, especially if we keep coming back to these points.

"I have a board meeting next Thursday, and I feel confident enough in my team to make a presentation to the board about the implications of the people side of business for the organization as a whole. They hired me to take Dominion in a new direction; I think it's time for me to unveil it for them."

"When we first got together," Tom said, "We told you that when we start a project, we want to be reasonably confident that we're working with someone with a real commitment to fundamental change. You said you were, and you were as good as your word. I think your board will be pleased with what they hear. Let's say we touch base again after the meeting."

"Sounds like a plan," Charlie said.

Selected Leadership Implications of the Six Principles

Principle 1: Accept people

- Accept people with their rational and nonrational features

- Engage with people on an emotional level

- Recognize that emotion preempts logic

- Speak with passion about the job and the organization

Principle 2: Nurture staff

- Actively care for your people

- Provide support and encouragement

- Ensure safety and security

- Connect with your people and avoid rejection

Principle 3: Create work families

- Create a family-like atmosphere in the workplace

- Treat all team members fairly, respectfully, and honestly

- Encourage trust and engagement

- Build and support teams

The Third Domain of Organizational Excellence

Principle 4: Encourage growth

- Encourage professional growth

- Set an example by taking advantage of growth opportunities yourself

- Encourage risk taking

- Ensure employees maintain an effective work-life balance

Principle 5: Build structure

- Make sure there are clear rules and performance standards

- Hold everyone equally accountable

- Assess performance not people

- Provide constructive feedback on performance

Principle 6: Embrace healthy diversity

- Appreciate your employees as individuals

- Adjust job descriptions to fit their strengths

- Embrace healthy diversity in all its aspects

- Deal firmly and fairly with counterproductive individuals

EPILOGUE

BUILDING THE PEOPLE
SIDE OF BUSINESS
INTO THE
ORGANIZATION

In the two months since the MRSA outbreak led Charlie Fisher to call an emergency meeting of his executive team, much has changed at Dominion. Thanks to Charlie's leadership, the executive team has begun to gel. A spirit of cooperation and collegiality has replaced the wariness, resentment, and territoriality that undermined its performance. The team has also committed to developing a leadership model based on six psychological principles distilled by Lee Hersch and Tom DeMaio. Dominion's executives have adopted this framework because they recognize that they cannot maximize performance without responding to how real people operate.

This new focus has already paid dividends. Charlie just received a note from Sally and Ryan indicating that preliminary analysis of the latest statistics shows that MRSA is on the wane. The outbreak was the result of a breakdown in the people side of Dominion's business, and the success in addressing it is, accordingly, a reflection of the organization's newfound cohesion. The two team members will give their status report on MRSA at the Friday executive team meeting.

Now it's Thursday, and Charlie is getting ready to make his presentation on the people side of business to Dominion's board of directors. His goal is to convey to them—as clearly and as emphatically as he can—how emphasizing the people side of business will make Dominion a different organization.

As is his habit, Charlie arrives at Dominion early. These days when he gets out of his car, it's dark out, and today Charlie notices a hint of fall in the air as he walks across the parking lot. Understandably, Charlie's a little nervous. When the board hired him, the members made it clear that they chose him because they wanted a new direction for Dominion. When he steps into the boardroom, he will stake his future and the future of the organization on his vision. He will ask the board to endorse his conception of Dominion as an organization that strives for excellence in the people side of business as well as in the technical and business domains. It will be a decisive moment in his tenure as CEO, the moment when he puts his mark on Dominion in much the same way that Jim Hawthorne did 20 years before.

Charlie's goal this morning is to run through his presentation one last time, reviewing the points he wants to make and anticipating the board's response. He had thought that he would begin by reviewing the six principles, but now he begins to shuffle his PowerPoint deck. "I might as well make it clear that this is what they've been waiting for," Charlie thinks to himself. He imagines himself addressing the board:

"When you began your search for a new CEO, you realized that Dominion was at a turning point. During his 20-year tenure, Jim Hawthorne, through sheer force of character and canny business sense, had reinvented Dominion, transforming it from a local hospital into a regional medical center. In many ways, Dominion was an extension of Jim's personality, and when Jim left, Dominion suffered.

"You brought me in not because you wanted another charismatic leader but because you wanted someone who would use Jim's achievement as a foundation for offering a broader, more encompassing vision of this organization, one that transcended individuals. The proposal I am about to put before you will do exactly that."

Charlie pauses for a second and reviews what he's said. "That's a good way to set things up," he thinks. "At this point, I should have their attention, and I've done so without criticizing Jim or Bob. So far, so good."

Charlie flips through his PowerPoint deck and settles on the first slide. His goal now is to introduce the people side of business. He takes his cue from his initial meeting with Tom and Lee and the introduction he made at the executive team retreat.

"There are three elements that contribute to the success of any business. First, there is the technical domain. In our case, it is the medical services we supply, but if we were a brokerage house, it would be financial services; if we were a chip maker, it would be our expertise in fabrication. Second, there is the business domain, which includes everything from strategic planning to finance to marketing and sales. I would give Dominion a B+ to A- in both areas."

THE THREE DOMAINS OF ORGANIZATIONAL EXCELLENCE

Charlie pauses for a second. "Would it be better to be less specific?" he asks himself. "Maybe something like 'Dominion has fallen short'"? He decides hard-hitting is better.

"As you know, on the medical side, we've been dealing with a MRSA outbreak that is surprising for an organization at our level of medical sophistication. On the business side, in the last year we've fallen short on our performance goals and we've been having a problem retaining nurses."

Charlie pauses and collects himself, before coming to his point. "I believe we've been having problems gaining traction in the medical and business areas because we've neglected the third domain, the people side of business. What's worse, we've not so much neglected it as we've been blind to it. We haven't considered the people side of what we do at all. Our medical staff can perform incredibly complex and delicate operations. Our administrative staff is adept at navigating Medicare and insurance reimbursements. Yet no one here has the knowledge to manage our people efficiently. We seem to feel two ways about it: We haven't taken a systematic approach because we feel people are too complex to understand, but at the same time, we dismiss managing people as irrelevant."

Charlie reconsiders. "That's all true, but I'm losing momentum," he thinks with a frown. "I need to cut to the chase."

He resumes: "It is my contention that our failure to attain excellence in the people side of business undermines our performance in the technical and business domains. It's at the root of the problems I've cited, and creates weaknesses in its own right, like our poor showing on patient satisfaction surveys. It is my goal to make excellence in the people side of business an organizational priority."

"That's more like it," Charlie thinks to himself. "I can't get much clearer. Now let's see if I can get them on the same page."

Charlie shifts gears. "People have always been my interest and my study. When I became a doctor, I choose to specialize in family medicine because it gave me an opportunity to work closely with people over the course of many years. The same type of interest led me to pursue a degree in business. I wanted to learn how to lead an organization, which fundamentally is a collection of people.

"I mention this because I found, on reflection, that even someone like me, someone already attuned to the people side of business, didn't really understand how people operated at work. Every part of what I do as a physician and as a leader requires me to understand people, yet I lacked a framework for doing so. That's why I brought in Lee Hersch and Tom DeMaio. These two consultants have developed a straightforward framework of six psychological principles that describes the way people act in an organization and why. It's the distillation of much research and experience, but it's straightforward. Here it is:

THE PEOPLE SIDE OF BUSINESS

SIX PSYCHOLOGICAL PRINCIPLES

1. The design of the brain determines human behavior.

2. People are most productive in an emotionally safe and supportive atmosphere.

3. People working together tend to replicate family structures and dynamics.

4. People want an opportunity for growth to achieve mastery.

5. People need structure to shape and motivate their behavior.

6. Individuals are different from one another.

Charlie imagines himself walking through the six principles, at this point second nature to him. He uses the first principle to set the stage, emphasizing the need to deal with human beings as they actually operate and providing the essential biology and evolutionary theory the board needs to grasp his point. As he moves through Principles 2, 3, 4, and 5, he stresses the human need for both support and structure. In his discussion of Principle 6, he underlines that the contours of human behavior allow ample room for variation as well as that harnessing diversity productively is a critical organizational challenge.

Having run through this review quickly in his mind, Charlie gets up from the desk and walks the circuit of his office. He needs to release a little energy, but he doesn't want to lose focus. He goes back to his desk and his PowerPoint.

"My priority over the next year is to re-create Dominion to reflect these principles. Some of the changes will be subtle, while others will be more dramatic, so I want to review with you some of the ways in which acting on these principles will change Dominion as an organization.

"How will Dominion be different? Let's start with Principle 1: *The design of the brain determines human behavior.* Dominion will be a place where we accept people as they are designed and where our managers and leaders will have the framework to deal with predictable human emotions and encourage those emotions that benefit the organization. This means that Dominion will both appreciate and foster such emotions as loyalty, passion, and commitment.

The Third Domain of Organizational Excellence

"How will Dominion be different when it has accepted the second principle, when it has implemented an atmosphere that reflects that *people are most productive in an emotionally safe and supportive environment?* For one thing, Dominion will be a place where we explicitly recognize the value of our staff, and where we are willing to act on that recognition by doing things like providing encouragement, reinforcement, and guidance. Nurturing and supporting staff—because it is in the best interests of the organization to do so—will be an explicit value of this company.

"Principle 3, which states that *people working together tend to replicate family structures and dynamics,* provides additional insight into how Dominion will change. We will emphasize teams as one way to productively manage people's innate tendency to impose family structure on groups. Dominion will be an organization that sees teams as its essential operational unit, that views teamwork as the process that drives it toward success, and that, accordingly, makes it a priority to build and support strong, fluid teams.

"Principle 4: *People want an opportunity for growth to achieve mastery,* highlights my vision for transforming Dominion. People want to grow and gain capacity. They want to bulk up mentally." Charlie stops for a second. "'Bulk up mentally'? Huh? Let's try that again."

"Principle 4: *People want an opportunity for growth to achieve mastery,* highlights my vision for transforming Dominion. People gain immense satisfaction from learning new ideas and from seeing things from new perspectives, and that satisfaction transfers to organizations that encourage their growth. As a result, Dominion will prize active learning and will make it safe for people to take risks as part of their search for mastery.

"Principle 5 is straightforward: *People need structure to shape and motivate their behavior.* As an organization, we will take our goals and expectations seriously. We will set them carefully, communicate them clearly, and hold ourselves collectively and individually accountable for realizing them.

"Principle 6 states that *individuals are different from one another.* As an organization, Dominion is going to do everything it can to encourage productive diversity of all kinds as the source of our competitive advantage."

Charlie decides that he won't show the summary slide until he finishes his rundown of the organizational implications of the six principles. He reviews that slide.

THE SIX PRINCIPLES: ORGANIZATIONAL IMPLICATIONS

Dominion will be a place where

1. We accept people as designed and where our managers and leaders will have the framework to deal with predictable human emotions and encourage those emotions that benefit the organization.

2. We explicitly recognize the value of our staff, and where we act on that recognition by providing encouragement, reinforcement, and guidance.

3. Teams are the essential operational unit, with teamwork seen as the process that drives success, and where it is it a priority to build and support strong, fluid teams.

4. Active learning is prized and where it is safe for people to take risks as part of their search for mastery.

5. Goals and expectations are set carefully and communicated clearly, and where we hold people accountable, individually and collectively, for realizing them.

6. We encourage productive diversity of all kinds as the source of our competitive advantage.

"Okay, we're in the home stretch," Charlie thinks to himself. "Now to pull this together for them." He chooses the next slide he intends to show:

BENEFITS FROM FOCUSING ON THE PEOPLE SIDE OF BUSINESS

1. Reaffirms the importance of our staff

2. Reinforces technical and business excellence

3. Improves customer satisfaction

4. Strengthens the Dominion brand

5. Supports the bottom line

Charlie imagines himself looking at each of the board members. "The advantages Dominion will gain by focusing on excellence in the people side of business will be substantial. For one thing, it affirms the indisputable truth that our staff is our most valuable asset. The knowledge and commitment each staff member brings to Dominion establishes our baseline as a company. The more knowledge and commitment they have, the more we can hope to achieve, so the benefits of making Dominion a more engaging and satisfying place to work cannot be underestimated.

"As I've said before, excellence in the people side of business is a prerequisite for true excellence in the medical and business domains. When staff feels supported, when they are encouraged to stretch and learn, and when they work to fulfill expectations that are clear and consistent, the quality of their work improves dramatically. Organizations achieve excellence in the technical and business domains only when the staff is committed to their mission and can attend fully to the task at hand. Such attention will also improve safety, because staff will make the effort to be extra vigilant. Safety is a function of a caring culture, not a rule-driven culture.

"Focusing on the people side of business not only affects an organization internally but it shapes its external relations, with customers as well as with vendors. In effect, when you have an internal culture that supports and sustains people, your external relationships will also reflect this orientation in terms of service and courtesy. Outstanding customer service will naturally flow as an extension of who we are as an organization.

The Third Domain of Organizational Excellence

"Focusing on the people side of business is also an effective way to strengthen the Dominion brand. Thanks to our reputation for providing high-quality advanced care, people come to Dominion when they are very sick. But that's not enough. We want people to know us as a place that treats them compassionately and considerately. Performing consistently and delivering on our promise will develop long-term relationships with our patients. We want people to turn to Dominion clinics like the one we're opening on the north side of town for their routine care and to come to the medical center for their more serious medical problems.

"This brings us to the last advantage: reinforcing our bottom line. Everything I've stressed so far—increasing staff productivity and satisfaction, improving technical and business performance, increasing customer satisfaction, strengthening our brand—affects our bottom line. Realigning our organization to address the people side of business is absolutely essential if we are to remain a profitable and successful enterprise."

Charlie thinks for a second. "How am I going to wrap this up? What am I really trying to say about how emphasizing the people side of business would change Dominion as an organization?" He sits in his chair and looks out over the parking lot. He has grown used to the view, and feels comfortable in his office with his poster hanging above the conference table. An idea strikes him. "I guess that will do," he says to himself.

"Ultimately," he says, resuming his imaginary speech. "Emphasizing the people side of business will make Dominion a place that nourishes people, that challenges them, that brings out their very best. It will be a place, quite rare these days, where people look forward to coming to work. An organization that can inspire these feelings in its staff is truly a powerful organization."

Charlie prints off a copy of his slides and stands up. He's ready to make the case for the people side of business and begin transforming the organizational culture at Dominion.

REFERENCES

Atkinson, B. (2005). *Emotional intelligence in couples therapy.* New York: W. W. Norton & Company.

Bennis, W. & Nanus , B. (1985). *Leaders: The strategies for taking charge.* New York: Harper & Row, Publishers.

Bennis, W. & Biederman, P. (1997). *Organizing Genius: The secret of creative collaboration.* Cambridge: Perseus Books.

Block, P. (1981). *Flawless consulting: A guide to getting your expertise used.* Amsterdam: Pfeiffer & Company.

Bowlby, J. (1969/1982). *Attachment and loss: Vol. 1. Attachment.* New York: Basic Books.

Bowlby, J. (1973). *Attachment and loss: Vol. 2. Separation: Anxiety and anger.* New York: Basic Books.

Bowlby, J. (1980). *Attachment and loss: Vol. 3. Loss: Sadness and depression.* New York: Basic Books.

Bowlby, J. (1988). *A secure base: Parent-child attachment and healthy human development.* New York: Basic Books.

Brafman, O. & Brafman , R. (2008). *Sway: The irresistible pull of irrational behavior.* New York: Doubleday.

Buckingham, M., & Clifton, D. (2001). *Now, discover your strengths*. New York: The Free Press.

Buckingham, M., & Coffman, C. (1999). *First, break all the rules*. New York: Simon & Schuster.

Buss, D.M. Ed. (2005). *The handbook of evolutionary psychology*. Hoboken: John Wiley & Sons, Inc.

Cassidy, J. & Shaver, P. (1999) *Handbook of attachment: Theory, research, and clinical applications*. New York: The Guilford Press.

Champy, J. & Nohria, N. (2000). *The arc of ambition: Defining the leadership journey*. Cambridge: Perseus Books.

Collins, J. (2001). *Good to great: Why some companies make the leap...and others don't*. New York: Harper Collins Publishers.

Covey, S. (1989). *The 7 habits of highly successful people: Powerful lessons in personal change*. New York: Fireside.

Daniels, A. (2000). *Bringing out the best in people*. New York: McGraw-Hill.

Deming, W. (1982). *Quality productivity and competitive position*. Cambridge: Massachusetts Institute of Technology Press.

Finney, M. (2008). *The truth about getting the best from people*. Upper Saddle River, NJ: FT Press.

Frankl, V. (1962). *Man's search for meaning*. New York: Washington Square Press.

Gallessich, J. (1982). *The profession and practice of consultation.* San Francisco: Jossey-Bass Publishers.

Gladwell, M. (2000). *The tipping point: How little things can make a big difference.* New York: Little, Brown and Company.

Goleman, D. (1994). *Emotional intelligence.* New York: Bantam Books.

Kotter, J. (2002). *The new rules: How to succeed in today's post corporate world.* Cambridge: Harvard Business School Press.

Lorsch, J. & Tierney, T. (2002): *Aligning the stars: How to succeed when professionals drive results.* Boston: Harvard Business School Press.

LeDoux, J. (1996). *The emotional brain.* New York: Simon & Schuster.

Lencioni, P. (2002). *The five dysfunctions of a team.* San Francisco: Jossey-Bass.

Maslow A. (1968). *Toward a psychology of being.* New York: John Wiley & Sons.

Maslow, A. (1970). *Motivation and personality.* New York: John Wiley & Sons.

Maslow A. (1998). *Maslow on management.* New York: John Wiley and Sons.

Maxwell, J. (1998). *The 21 irrefutable laws of leadership: Follow them and people will follow you.* Nashville: Thomas Nelson.

Neusch, D. & Siebenaler, A. (1998). *The high performance enterprise: Reinventing the people side of your business.* New York: John Wiley & Sons.

Pickering, J., Brokaw, G., Harnden, P., & Gardner, A. (2005). *Building high-performance organizations in the twenty-first century.* Charlottesville, VA: Commonwealth Center for High Performance Organizations, Inc. (www.highperformanceorg.com).

Rosen, R. (1991). The *healthy company: Eight strategies to develop people, productivity, and profits.* New York: G.P. Putnam's Sons.

Selye, H. (1975). *The stress of life.* New York: McGraw Hill.

Spradlin, W. & Porterfield, P. (1979). *Human biosociology: From cell to culture.* New York: Springer-Verlag.

Studer, Q. (2003). *Hardwiring excellence.* Gulf Breeze, FL: Fire Starter Publishing.

Studer, Q. (2008). *Results that last: hardwiring behaviors that will take your company to the top.* Hoboken, NJ: John Wiley & Sons.

Watzlawick, P., Weakland, J., & Fisch, R. (1974). *Change: Principles of problem formation and problem resolution.* New York: W. W. Norton.

Willingham, R. (1997). *The people principle: A revolutionary redefinition of leadership.* New York: St. Martin's Press.

ABOUT THE AUTHORS

Tom DeMaio and Lee Hersch have each spent the last three decades applying the insights of psychology to business and public policy. Both Tom and Lee are clinical psychologists and organizational consultants, who supervise other psychologists, lead in their national professional associations, participate as University faculty members, and serve on community boards and commissions. They live in the central Virginia area and can be reached at HerschDeMaio.com.

Made in the USA
Charleston, SC
20 July 2012